**Personnel Needs
and Changing
Reference
Service**

For my mother for her love, patience, and ever constant willingness to forego the sound of music for the sound of a printer.

Personnel Needs and Changing Reference Service

Rosemarie Riechel

Library
Professional
Publications
1989

Copyright © 1989 Rosemarie Riechel
All rights reserved.
First published in 1989 as a
Library Professional Publication, an imprint of
The Shoe String Press, Inc.,
Hamden, Connecticut 06514

Printed in the United States of America

Library of Congress Cataloging-in-Publication Data
Riechel, Rosemarie, 1937–
  Personnel needs and changing reference service /
Rosemarie Riechel.
    p. cm.
    Bibliography: p.
    Includes index.
    ISBN 0–208–02226–0. —ISBN 0–208–02227–9 (pbk.)
    1. Reference librarians. 2. Library personnel
management. 3. Reference services (Libraries)—
Management. I. Title.
Z682.4.R44R53 1989
025.04—dc20   89–8091
                                             CIP

Contents

Preface ix

Introduction 1

1 **The Information Specialist Defined** 7
   Recommended Sources 10

2 **Reference Personnel Training and Development** 13
   General Orientation and Training 15
   Evaluating Service 18
   The Reference Interview 18
   Online Searchers and Online Searching 24
   Selected Automated Systems and Services 26
   Training for the Search Process 39
   Glossary of Computer Terminology 42
   Sample Staff Development Sessions 46
   Educating the End-User 50

3 **Case Studies** 57
   List of Sources Cited 90

4 **Evaluating Reference** 94
   The Staff 97
   The Resources 104

Bibliography 109

Index 117

Preface

Concern about the impact of technology on reference service began almost two decades ago and is still a major issue today. For the most part, librarians have come to realize that they will not be replaced by computers. Rather, the continuing growth of online database systems and services has led to considerable need for experts who can efficiently retrieve all sorts of information as well as develop methods of teaching new reference skills to both staff and patrons.

The premise of this book is that instead of resisting change, by using budget constraints and time and staff shortages as excuses, professionals should actively and wholeheartedly embrace the concept of the librarian as information specialist, teacher, trainer, and counselor. Attention to new personnel needs is essential to the achievement of quality reference work.

This book is intended to be a handbook of essential information and a practical guide for the improvement of reference service. It is born out of my own evolution from traditional reference librarian to researcher, online search specialist, educator, and trainer of staff and patrons.

I wish to express my gratitude to my colleagues for the information they so willingly shared; and to Susan Hess, Juan Morel Campos IS71 Junior High School, for her cooperation and contribution of material on the use of the ELECTRONIC ENCYCLOPEDIA.

I owe a special debt of gratitude to my brother, Donald C. Riechel, Ohio State University, for his support and valuable help.

Introduction

There is certainly no lack of available reference resources and means of access to information that cover a wide variety of subject areas and patron interests. However, many libraries are unable to acquire specialized manual sources or to add and integrate automated systems into their present resources. This is the result of administrative decisions, budget limitations, insufficient staff, or personnel with inadequate knowledge, skill, interest, and motivation for the job. Generally, librarians agree that automated retrieval systems have changed the shape and scope of reference service. They recognize the fact that people require, expect, and demand more from their libraries because information needs have become more complex. While a significant number of academic, corporate, public, and special libraries *have* responded positively, and successfully, to user requirements, too many are not living up to patron expectations because of unrecognized and unfulfilled staffing needs. Also, many librarians cannot accommodate the wider interests evinced by users because they have failed to step back and look at themselves in relation to the service they provide. It is vital that they come to grips with the need to become technology literate and skilled in the automated searching process, in order to deal effectively with one of modern society's dilemmas—how to get an overload of information to the growing and diverse number of persons who need it, supplying also some selection and sorting assistance.

Since the primary function of reference service is to fulfill user needs, reference librarians and library administrators, regardless of type of library, must recognize the importance of total inte-

2 / **Introduction**

gration of automated information retrieval systems into the reference function. This requires the allocation of funds, personnel, and staff support programs necessary to make electronic tools as accessible as any other information resource. Computers are growing increasingly popular for efficiently storing, finding, and selectively retrieving data from a vast sea of information. Users of information include researchers, scholars, college, high school, and elementary school students, professionals, business executives, entrepreneurs, politicians, generalists, trivia buffs, and many other categories. Despite the attractiveness of the personal computer and the initial lure of do-it-yourself searching, the majority of information seekers usually must depend, for extensive or sophisticated searching, on information providers/intermediary searchers/consultants, who have a knowledge of complex systems. Such intermediaries should have the expertise to retrieve the data sought, and the talent to explain or teach the process to users. It is high time for skilled information specialists to replace the old guardians of the realm and keepers of the gate who may be inclined to limit or deny access to electronic databases for a variety of shaky reasons, including the following:

1. *Budget:* Online systems and microcomputer hardware and software are too expensive and it takes time to justify requests for additional funding to support expanding such systems; also, there will be an increased demand for periodicals and books not in the collection that will put a strain on an already insufficient budget; there are so many new automated systems and products available that it is impossible to satisfy all patron demands.
2. *Time/staff:* A great amount of time is used just showing patrons how to use the catalog (now frequently automated) so staff cannot be bothered with other teaching tasks; too much time has to be spent on either doing the searching for patrons, showing them how to use the system(s), or monitoring the equipment, so that other people with traditional

reference questions would be shortchanged; librarians are not teachers and do not have the time for such a labor-intensive job; staff does not have the time to learn how to use different systems because they are too busy answering questions and maintaining the collection; there is no time, given a limited, busy staff, to counsel patrons on searching techniques and how to achieve better results when they are doing it themselves on their home or office computers.

3. *User's age:* High school, junior high school or elementary school students are frequently barred because their requests are considered frivolous; their (unimportant) information needs can be satisfied by searching hard copy sources; they are too young to be engaged in serious research; they are seeking the easy way out of a homework assignment; they are too young to make good use of the data retrieved via more complex and nontraditional tools.

4. *Academic achievement of user:* Undergraduate assignments are not complex enough to warrant the use of specialized and sophisticated tools; term paper assignments are designed to make the student use only traditional sources; community college and college work is supposed to be time-consuming to be valid; asking a librarian to assist in finding information quickly makes the completion of the assignment less valid.

5. *Personal judgment of the significance of the data sought:* The query may be deemed trivial if the person is seeking a newspaper article that names a restaurant famous for blueberry cheese cake, magazine stories about Elvis Presley, or any other information that does not fit into the category of "serious" research, as defined by the librarian.

6. *The user has no time to visit the library to conduct research:* Telephoning patrons are not entitled to online service since searches on sophisticated systems should only be conducted when the patron is present; a telephoned request is most probably frivolous and indicates only casual need.

7. *Providing access to online databases is a privilege:* Scientists, re-

searchers, and faculty have the inalienable right to take advantage of technology since databases were actually developed to store and retrieve scholarly and technical data.
8. *Online information retrieval is expensive:* The cost of searching has to be recovered fully or partially from the user; those who cannot afford the fee should be excluded from using the service.

Today's reference librarian should no longer be trapped in the narrow role of custodian and tollgate keeper—charging admission (in still too many cases) for access to so-called "special" services. Users of any type of library (academic, public, corporate, special) should not be forced to travel the more difficult routes to information, or be confined to the limited collections of their own libraries for any reason. Online systems expand collections beyond the walls of individual libraries and provide access to a variety of general and specialized databases. Anyone living in this information society—laypersons, students, businessmen, scientists, entrepreneurs, researchers, professionals, and more—should be able to take advantage of automated retrieval systems because of the benefits they offer:

- Current information as well as obscure data are quickly located and retrieved.
- Complex searches can be conducted easily by linking concepts.
- Time-consuming multiple look-ups in hard copy indexes are no longer necessary in many instances.
- Comprehensive bibliographic searches can be completed rapidly.
- Tailor-made bibliographies can be quickly created, allowing the user more time to study the source material.
- The full text of documents, not readily available to the reader, can be easily printed, providing an efficient alternative to interlibrary loan.
- Information not otherwise available, such as wire service sto-

ries, or material from databases with no printed counterparts, is accessible.
- Searching by key word, word stems, word proximity, and fields of bibliographic information (in the records) makes the likelihood of successful data retrieval greater.
- Information or bibliographies on specific topic(s) can be quickly updated with a date limitation or by using an SDI (Selective Dissemination of Information) service, whereby search strategies are saved indefinitely and run automatically each time the selected databases are updated.
- Menu-driven or simplified command systems designed with the novice in mind can be searched for less complex information, such as specific facts, names, dates, and bibliographic citations.
- When patrons conduct their own searches, immediate retrieval of certain data is possible, without the usual waiting time of a day, a week, or more that is required for mediated searching by librarians.

If the use of print and electronic sources is to be freely enjoyed by all users, librarians should provide full service to both independent searchers and the more dependent ones. The former want access to electronic tools to be just as easy as it is to go to the shelves for print material, and the latter expect the librarian either to hand-hold or to actually do the bulk of the work of data retrieval.

When the help, guidance, and support of an intermediary searcher/information consultant/experienced reference librarian is required, will users be able to find such a person at reference desks? Are reference managers and administrators taking a hard look at reference service and what is being done to get the staff qualified to provide quality service? Library literature abounds with discussions of new developments in information technology and ways in which the traditional role of the reference librarian has changed, but minimal attention has been paid to evaluating

6 / Introduction

automated information retrieval service and identifying updated requirements in staff skills and abilities. Because the lack of competent information specialists guarantees mediocre service, it is time to define clearly the expanding role of the reference librarian—as information specialist and educator—and to identify personnel requirements and training needs.

1
The Information Specialist Defined

If they are to avoid obsolescence or professional atrophy, today's reference librarians must recognize that knowledge of computers, automated systems, and online retrieval skills is as essential to effective service as is a solid background in traditional reference and research. Professionals should take personal responsibility for their learning. Quite often, attitudes and philosophies of service need revision in order to achieve the skills necessary to successfully retrieve information. These include conducting complex online searches, guiding patrons through the searching process, instructing them in the use of print or automated tools, or showing them the way to other libraries and resources when the collection and available databases prove inadequate.

A concentrated and consistent effort to read the literature, either at the workplace or elsewhere, is an effective way of keeping up with new developments and reference practices. Also, attendance at general, specialized, and advanced seminars, sponsored by database vendor services, libraries, cooperatives, networks, or other professional organizations, provides a quick update on reference issues and technological developments, and makes enhancement of particular automated systems and services possible and even pleasurable. Annual national and state library association conventions, as well as specialized meetings geared to the online industry, pack a year's worth of information on new technology and products into just a few days. It is a "listening-intensive" experience, but one does come away with a broad overview of trends and evolving technologies. Of course, an added

8 / Personnel Needs and Changing Reference Service

benefit is the opportunity to actually try out new products and talk with the people involved in their development. Information specialists are supposed to facilitate the access routes to information for all patrons, whatever their query. So, the specific needs, abilities, interests, demands, and communication skills of individual users must be assessed in order to tailor-make the information retrieval method for each. Just what does it take to successfully operate the reference desk in this more complex environment? When combined, the attributes and characteristics listed here constitute the portrait of an ideal reference librarian and true information specialist:

- in-depth knowledge of basic reference skills
- ability to identify new personal needs, skills, and abilities
- flexibility—quick acceptance of and adjustment to change
- enthusiasm for new technologies and the willingness to detach oneself sufficiently from a favorite online system to learn about others that are also important to users
- knowledge of the principles of online searching
- expertise in quickly ferreting out information using automated sources, manual sources, or both
- excellent human-to-human communication skills—helping the patron by responding readily and revealing all that is necessary to aid the information retrieval process
- ability to interact well with machines and fully understand the action of the hardware and software—along with the ability to handle problems skillfully
- talent for translating a request into terminology that results in efficient searching and rapid retrieval
- unflagging enthusiasm for the information hunt
- imaginative flair for thinking of efficient access routes to information, even if they are not at first obvious
- determination characteristic of an excellent and experienced reference librarian to deal evenhandedly with each patron and treat queries with the same attention, regardless of the perceived importance of the question

Information Specialist Defined / 9

- in-depth knowledge of the resources of other libraries and outside agencies
- total commitment to locating data within a particular library's collection or using the resources of other libraries, networks, and cooperatives
- ability to think logically, analytically, and in the abstract
- ability to identify synonyms, variant terms, or concepts
- skill in redefining concepts to achieve precision and maximum relevant recall
- patience and perseverance
- intelligence and imagination
- natural inclination for organization
- superb sense of humor and the ability to laugh at oneself and with users
- total commitment to and enjoyment of the process of information retrieval

Librarians have various backgrounds and different levels of knowledge, experience, expertise, and commitment to reference work. Various types of professionals might be described as follows:

- an experienced reference librarian with a talent for communicating with people and easily establishing rapport with patrons but with little knowledge of things computerized and a fear of the unknown—including the new online catalog
- an experienced professional frustrated by the inability to grasp the principles of online searching and no hands-on experience with simplified automated systems
- a talented professional with a negative attitude toward automated systems because of bad experiences with automated teller systems and the like
- a staff member who resists change and reminisces about the "good old days" of printed indexes and card catalogs
- a reference librarian who took a short course on microcomputer applications and is convinced that all it takes is to sit

down, press the "enter" key and magically retrieve all sorts of data—thus eliminating thinking before beginning the information retrieval process
- the new librarian who avoided "tough" computer courses and has minimal understanding of automated retrieval systems
- a highly motivated, experienced professional, with minimal formal training in online systems but a sound understanding of their capabilities and a strong desire to gain expertise via hands-on experience
- a professional with an in-depth knowledge of one vendor system and minimal motivation to learn how to operate others
- a skilled reference librarian who uses the collection and the resources of other libraries intelligently but is somewhat deficient in communication skills

Clearly, not all professionals have what it takes to be ideal information specialists, but librarians must be deeply involved in the process of personal growth and development. The quality of reference service depends upon it.

Recommended Sources

Much has been published recently that is valuable to reference librarians/information specialists. The following list of books and journals is useful for keeping up-to-date on reference service, online service, and technological developments. It is not all-inclusive but is intended as a basic guide to important source material. To keep current on newly published titles, the book review sections in many of the journals listed below should be examined.

Books

Answers Online: Your Guide to Information Data Bases. Barbara Newlin. Berkeley, Calif.: Osborne McGraw-Hill, 1985.

Complete Handbook of Personal Computer Communications. Alfred Glossbrenner. New York: St. Martin's, 1985.

Databases: Primer for Retrieving Information by Computer. Susanne Humphrey and Biagio John Melloni. Englewood Cliffs, N.J.: Prentice-Hall, 1986.

Developing Computer-Based Library Systems. John Corbin. Phoenix, Ariz.: Oryx Press, 1981.

Education for Professional Librarians. Herbert S. White, ed. White Plains, N.Y.: Knowledge Industry, 1986.

End-User Searching: Services and Providers. Martin Kesselman and Sarah B. Watstein, eds. Chicago: American Library Association, 1988.

How to Look it Up Online. Alfred Glossbrenner. New York: St. Martin's, 1987.

Improving Telephone Information and Reference Service in Public Libraries. Rosemarie Riechel. Hamden, Conn.: Library Professional Publications, 1987.

Introduction to Reference Work. 2 vols. 4th ed. William A. Katz. New York: McGraw-Hill, 1982.

Librarian's Guide to Telephone Reference Service. Rochelle Yates. Hamden, Conn.: Library Professional Publications, 1986.

Managing Online Reference Services. Ethel Auster, ed. New York: Neal-Schuman, 1986.

Microcomputer User's Guide to Information Online. Carol Hansen. Hasbrouck Heights, N.J.: Hayden, 1984.

Online Reference and Information Retrieval. 2nd ed. Roger C. Palmer. Littleton, Colo.: Libraries Unlimited, 1987.

Online Retrieval: Analysis and Strategy. Peter J. Vigil. New York: Wiley, 1988.

Reference and Information Services: A Reader for Today. Bill Katz, ed. and comp. Metuchen, N.J.: Scarecrow, 1986.

12 / **Personnel Needs and Changing Reference Service**

Reference Services and Library Instruction: A Handbook for Library Management. David F. Kohl. Santa Barbara, Calif.: ABC-CLIO, 1985.

Reference Work in the Public Library. Rolland E. Stevens and Joan M. Walton. Littleton, Colo.: Libraries Unlimited, 1983.

Reference Work in the University Library. Rolland E. Stevens and Linda C. Smith. Littleton, Colo.: Libraries Unlimited, 1987.

Smarter Telecommunications. Charles Bowen. New York: Bantam, 1985.

Success in Answering Reference Questions: Two Studies. Frances Benham and Ronald R. Powel. Metuchen, N.J.: Scarecrow, 1987.

Journals

Bulletin of the American Society for Information Science. Bimonthly. Washington, D.C.: American Society for Information Science, 1974–.

DATABASE. Bimonthly. Weston, Conn.: Online, Inc., 1978–.

Database User. Monthly. Westport, Conn.: Meckler, 1985–.

Information Technology and Libraries. Quarterly. Chicago: American Library Association, 1982–.

Information Today: The Newspaper for Users and Producers of Electronic Information Services. Monthly. Medford, N.J.: Learned Information, 1983–.

InfoWorld. Weekly. Pasadena, Calif.: InfoWorld, 1980–.

Library Hi Tech. Quarterly. Ann Arbor, Mich.: 1983–.

Link-Up: The News Magazine for Users of Online Services. Bimonthly. Medford, N.J.: Learned Information, 1983–.

ONLINE. Bimonthly. Weston, Conn.: Online, Inc., 1976–.

Online Review. Bimonthly. Medford, N.J.: Learned Information, 1977–.

Reference Librarian. Semi-annual. New York: Haworth, 1981–.

RQ. Quarterly. Chicago: Reference and Adult Services Division, American Library Association, 1960–.

Small Computers in Libraries. Monthly. Westport, Conn.: Meckler, 1981–.

2
Reference Personnel Training and Development

Some argue that staff development and training programs are costly and time-consuming processes that are not worth the effort. Those who object the loudest are usually the ones who do not consider reference service a priority. As a result, they do not take a good look at what is going on at reference desks and neglect to seek answers to some important questions, such as:

1. Are library users given access to a wide variety of hard copy sources as well as the option of online database searching?
2. Is intermediary searching readily available and is it done skillfully and correctly?
3. Are automated systems designed for end-user searching available and are information and instruction given when requested?
4. Does the staff have enough time to spend on complex requests, lengthy reference interviews, counseling, and instructional sessions?
5. Are the librarians expert information specialists who can easily suggest alternative routes to information that would be more efficient, yield better results, or enhance what has already been retrieved?
6. Does the staff leave the reference desk to go to the catalog, the books, or the microcomputers with the patron?
7. If the information is not available in the library, does the staff know of other libraries or information resources and readily refer the patron to them?

8. Is there sufficient qualified staff available to provide quality service and serve all users with equal interest?

If librarians, reference/information managers, and administrators assume that all is well because circulation figures are high, patrons do not complain, and everybody always looks busy, then they have not closely examined personnel needs or the library's responsibility for ensuring that quality reference service is being provided. In too many cases, staff education and training are not viewed as functions of the employing library. Undeniably, library schools and library associations do play an important role in the education of professionals, and individual staff members have to be inescapably involved in their own professional development process. But the employing library must also do its share by developing formal in-house training and instruction programs for every staff member. This is essential to the provision of quality service.

The constant stream of new electronic developments, such as system enhancements, hardware and software improvements, new databases, and simplified methods of searching them, makes ongoing training programs imperative. The process of creating different types of training sessions to accommodate an assortment of informational needs for a variety of people with different degrees of knowledge, various learning rates, and levels of understanding is labor-intensive, costly, and time-consuming. But it is worth the effort if knowledge of reference techniques is deepened, fear of technology is lessened, resistance to change is defeated, knowledge of online searching is gained or increased, understanding of the principles of automated systems and knowledge of particular services is improved, rapport with patrons is increased, the percentage of correct answers is greater, and the ability to accurately recall information from electronic resources is increased.

Specific staff training, development, and orientation programs that can be adapted for use in any type of library, regardless of size or population served, are outlined here. They are useful as practical guides for those who decide to develop such programs, for librarians who want to create an individualized plan of action, and for managers and administrators who want to get more deeply involved in the personnel nurturing process.

General Orientation and Training

General orientation programs should not be one-time occurrences that take place only when a new service or product is introduced or when new staff members are hired. Rather, they should be repeated regularly for the benefit of both new and existing staff in order to ensure that everyone remains up-to-date on procedures, activities, resources, and so forth.

General orientation sessions should be planned as soon as new staff arrive or changes occur in the library. These sessions should continue for as long as it takes the personnel involved to gain the knowledge and confidence to actively become a part of the reference team. They should include the following elements.

Philosophy of Service

An explication of the goals and objectives of the library and the fact that the expected high level of performance of the staff is basic to good service. The main function and varied roles of the library must be defined. For example, a public library serves as the center of information for an entire population, as well as an adult learning center, and should respond to all patron needs by providing free access to all available resources; an academic library exists to support the educational process, the curriculum, and research by providing access to primary and secondary source materials; the special library's function is to support the specific information needs of its institution's business or mission—medical, legal, corporate, etc.—by maintaining a complete and current collection in specific subject area(s) for its staff. In all situations, personnel is expected to know the collection thoroughly, to be able to determine when it is appropriate to use hard copy or automated tools (or a combination of both), and to have the expertise to retrieve correct and complete information from all sources, whatever the format might be. An in-depth knowledge of outside resources, such as other libraries, cooperatives, networks, and community agencies, is imperative, since patrons used to a responsive, thinking staff, will tend to ask all sorts of questions that might not be answered, or resolved fully in their particular libraries. A liberal referral policy that is not confined to community information type questions alone must be fully understood and closely followed by all personnel. It should be very clear that there is no room for "setter" librarians, those who just "set" and point! Rather, a vital, active, thinking, and cooperative team is what is required in order to fulfill the goals and functions of individual libraries.

Physical Arrangement of the Library

The location of the public catalog, the general reference desks, the subject departments, media centers, online services, public access computers and services, special collections/automated systems available, book collection(s), and special files should be covered by a complete tour of the building. The usual fast, superficial, large group tour is practically worthless. Following a general introduction to the facilities, individuals should be assigned to an experienced professional in each area in order to gain more in-depth knowledge of the resources and operation of each area.

Who is Who, Where is What and When

In order for staff to make intelligent decisions and referrals, those in charge of particular departments and services (i.e., subject specialists, online search intermediaries) should be introduced.

Also, a list of departments, branches, cooperating libraries, regional or central libraries, networks, and their special services/collections is essential. The telephone numbers, names of coordinators, supervisors, contact persons, and hours of service, should, of course, be included.

Automated Systems and Services

Back in the card catalog days it was sufficient to point it out, test filing skills and knowledge of rules and AACR II changes. But online or CD-ROM catalogs are becoming increasingly more common. Since the arrangement and operation of the different products vary, staff must gain an intimate knowledge of a library's primary finding tool—the equipment used, keyboard arrangement, the features, such as menu screens, function keys, search protocol, Boolean searching, delimiters (language, date, field, etc.), how to save or print records, and so forth.

There must be introduction to and demonstration of end-user systems. Individual staff members should be given the time to learn how to use these systems so that they can conduct competent mediated searches themselves or instruct patrons to do their own searches when they choose to.

Since professionals are expected to know the entire collection and make decisions concerning the best means of access to the information sought, the online intermediary search service must be explained in detail—what vendor systems are used, the type and number of databases available, the subjects covered, the procedure for initiating a search, translating the request into a search statement, etc. All reference librarians might not conduct mediated searches on complex systems, but they must know policy and procedure: residency requirements; limitations (such as time spent per search, number of records provided, number of databases searched per request); turn-around time per request; whether or not appointments are necessary; if patron's presence is required; if telephoned requests are accepted; method used to deliver the results to patrons, and so forth.

Demonstrations of the operation of all automated systems are as important as good manuals are to the reinforcement of what has been said and seen. A policy and procedure manual, preferably computer-produced and in loose-leaf format for quick and easy updating, should clearly and concisely outline the specifics of each automated system and service.

Evaluating Service

The importance of keeping accurate statistical records and factual reports must be emphasized—and reemphasized on a regular basis so that the job of evaluating reference service is made less difficult. If everyone takes the task seriously, justification of funding for additional staff and automated systems is that much more likely. The particular records kept, i.e., number of searches run and when, number of positive or negative results, time spent per search, print materials/databases searched—as well as how they are used—should be explained. Sample reports should be discussed, along with the impact they have on reference service.

General orientation sessions must be as thorough as possible so that reference service is not compromised by poorly informed personnel. Of course, such sessions should also include job descriptions, expected behavior when dealing with patrons (thoroughness of the reference interview, completeness of the answer, etc.), and routines such as answering the telephone, and juggling the telephoning patron with the in-person user, the complex queries with the ready-reference questions, time at the desk with time to learn and observe experienced staff.

The Reference Interview

Responses to ready-reference questions are usually swift, routine, and impersonal, because little effort is required to discover the patron's real need. But a stated request, although seemingly simple, might also be the patron's perception of what will yield an answer to a question or what is believed to be the limit of what the librarian will accept. With further interviewing, the librarian should discover the real need—perhaps the solution of a problem for which a better approach exists. A person asking for library hours may in fact be masking a need for material available in another department of the university or large public library; a question about a specific title or author (not located in the catalog) might, if the librarian probes correctly, reveal the need for help in clarifying a research problem or gaining information about the library's collection or automated retrieval systems. If the needed title is not held by the library, informing the patron of this fact should not end the reference transaction. Patrons often request material they mistakenly believe provides the information they seek. Using a personal approach, the librarian should be able to discover that the patron's real need is for any book on a particular subject.

Some people are not comfortable talking about their problems or voicing their needs to a person they do not know. The necessity for admitting ignorance or befuddlement about a subject, assignment, or concept frequently causes a patron to be vague or ambiguous—sometimes because the information was received secondhand or the subject is not fully understood. It is incumbent upon the librarian, as an information specialist, to determine what is really sought, to deliver accurate responses, and skillfully guide the patron through the retrieval process. If, on the other hand, the user wants to look for the data independently, clear instructions should be given on how to approach the particular search problem and how to use the print or automated sources.

Since library users generally expect that they will get expert help at the reference desk, it is imperative that the staff show interest in each query, quickly establish rapport with the patron(s), satisfy needs correctly and completely, and encourage continued use of the library as the primary source for information. Most professionals are aware that question negotiation is a difficult task but many all too often fall short of being astute and interested enough to try to "read" user needs by observing behavior—body language, facial expression, and tone of voice—while deciding on the best way to probe for pertinent information and clarification of the query. A librarian who is approachable, empathetic, interested, and patient can encourage people to talk about their information needs, why they are looking for certain data, and what level of information is required. A friendly attitude, devoid of any judgmental quality in connection with the questioner or the question(s) asked is always desirable and helpful in most cases. For example, a public librarian's response to a young man's question about what one writes on a postcard should be helpful and straightforward. On the surface, it seems a stupid question, but any hint of this judgment could lose an already shy and embarrassed questioner—who, as it turns out, is a foreign exchange student away from home for the first time.

"I know I'm in the wrong place, but I'll ask a silly question anyway. What exactly is a couch potato?" This patron, a chemist, should be assured by the librarian at the desk in the chemical company's library that no question is silly and that every effort will be made to get the information quickly. A friendly remark about the unique expression relieves embarrassment. Also, an immediate call to the local public library for a definition from a slang dictionary results in a satisfied patron.

The student with a homework assignment should be dealt with constructively so that the child's experience (in the school or public library) is a positive one. A lazy, lost or underachieving student, who either comes to the reference desk or wanders about the room aimlessly, stopping occasionally to flip through the pages of different books, needs attention. The librarian must probe, stimulate, and lead the child to the information, while giving a lesson in the use of the collection and the fun of looking for information. Computers and CD-ROM products designed for young students do motivate and are becoming more common in libraries. They should be available to children as well as adults as research and learning tools.

Establishing trust, as well as confidence, is an important aspect of the reference interview. Many people, particularly public library users, approach the reference desk seeking help with personal problems. Staff must recognize that, for most, this takes courage. It is therefore important to quickly put patrons at ease and to assure them that they made a good decision to come to the library for help. Every effort should be made either to solve the problem or to make a referral to another library or outside agency. If the patron expresses concern about calling the referral agency, the librarian should offer to do so, an action which shows sustained and sincere interest in the patron and the resolution of the problem.

Elderly people require special attention because they are frequently uninformed about where to go to solve personal problems. A concerned attitude and carefully worded questions should allow them to open up and explain what the real need is, i.e., a social security problem, a medical concern, a consumer complaint. Assurance that the information they give is kept confidential will often lead to the disclosure of additional details needed either to provide the correct information or a proper referral.

A good reference interview should conclude by encouraging the patron to come back if any other problems or questions arise. This reinforces trust and makes the next session with the patron easier to conduct.

Many requests for online searches begin as reference questions which cannot be answered fully, if at all, using the library's collection. Frequently the patron has difficulty pinpointing what is really sought. As a result, the query statement is ambiguous, brief and cryptic. The following are some examples:

"I'm looking for information about an epidemic in Nicaragua."

With further questioning, the librarian discovered that the patron was looking for recent newspaper articles on the dengue fever epidemic (caused by mosquitoes) that killed many people in Nicaragua. The fastest way to this information was via an online search.

"I'm looking for something on the quilted giraffe."

The patron, however, did not reveal that the Quilted Giraffe is a restaurant in New York City or that what was really sought was a review that appeared in the *New York Times* in 1987 or 1988. A NEXIS search in the NYT (NEW YORK TIMES FULL TEXT) file was indicated once the query was clarified.

"What are the effects on humans of toxic waste in the ocean?"

To clarify, the patron needed recent newspaper and wire service stories on the toxic waste problem in New Jersey, California, Scandinavia, (especially Denmark), and Antarctica. The researcher had not found enough material using printed indexes or INFOTRAC, and really wanted an online search.

Certain guidelines should be followed in order to determine if a user's needs would best be satisfied by using automated information retrieval resources:

1. Carefully interview the patron to determine the actual need, the context of the request, the subject areas involved, the specifics, whether any attempt has been made to obtain the information, the sources that were checked, and the terms that were used in the attempt to locate the data needed.
2. Consider all the possible sources for the needed data. Is some or all of the information available in hard copy sources in the collection—monographs, dictionaries, indexes, newspapers, pamphlets, and so forth? Is the material too recent or too obscure to be located without using online databases? Is only the most current information desired? Would printed sources or CD-ROM databases fail because they are not updated as frequently as online databases?

3. Decide on the best approach to the needed data. Is the patron combining two or more concepts into one question? Would full-text databases, using key words, be the most efficient way to get at the information? Are some of the data easily retrieved from printed indexes or CD-ROM databases, or is the use of online databases the best route to take? Does the patron want to do the searching—in printed sources and/or automated systems? If so, has the librarian explained the content, arrangement, means of access, and limitations of these tools?

Once an automated system has been selected, further interviewing must follow, using some sort of search strategy worksheet to write down all the pertinent data as well as key words, concepts, thesaurus terms, modifiers, etc.

Close interaction with the patron is crucial during the process of defining the search, translating the query statement into searchable terms, formulating the search strategy, selecting the appropriate systems and databases, and retrieving the information—or instructing the patron about how to do it. The librarian should not hesitate to admit ignorance about a subject, a term, or a concept. It is desirable for the faculty member, doctor, researcher, corporate executive, or whomever to be asked to explain the topic or define terms. A more precise search session is possible when users are encouraged to elaborate, clarify, and supply alternative words or phrases. Also, asking youngsters and students to describe what they are looking for encourages them to think and involves them in a positive learning experience.

A post-search interview should follow the information retrieval process. The results of the search should be discussed to be sure that the data retrieved completely answers the query and satisfies the patron.

Of course, a previous positive experience on the part of the patron is valuable because then the interview routine is familiar. The patron should be encouraged to learn to come better prepared by defining terms and working out strategies before starting to search independently or requesting a search at the reference desk. Training staff in the art of interviewing should include a combination of individualized tutoring, observation, and working with an experienced professional and mentor. Interview techniques and approaches to individual requests should be monitored and search strategies and results analyzed. Exercises, using actual questions, and particularly, unsuccessful searches, difficult requests for obscure data, and failed online searches should be part of training. Through this process the staff has the opportunity to analyze the interview process and the outcomes of individual transactions. At the same time, methods of improving interview technique and search strategy can be identified and discussed.

Just as patrons should not be judged by the questions they ask, staff should feel free to communicate with their supervisors and mentors and seek advice without fear of being judged. The effectiveness of the interview with the patron is totally dependent upon successful communication, and it should be modeled, with the interest and warmth that characterize it, by those who train and develop one staff's capabilities.

Online Searchers and Online Searching

Libraries are acquiring an increasing variety of computerized tools, ranging from CD-ROM catalogs and bibliographic databases to direct access database systems. At the high end of the product scale, complexity of use and the price tag will mandate the continued need for an expert online intermediary searcher. Other systems, designed to simplify the search process and encourage novices to do their own search, are more or less easy to use but, for the most part, some instruction in the mechanics of operation, the command language and database content is necessary. Generally, patron online search skills are poor. They tend to skip the process of defining a search and preparing the strategy before sitting down at the microcomputer—running the risk of retrieving no data, irrelevant material, or inaccurate information. When entering search statements, many do not read the on-screen instructions or carefully follow the menus and, as a result, do some odd things that lead to frustration. For example, a patron searching a CD-ROM catalog, specifically Bibliophile's Intelligent Catalog, might ignore the instructions to elect to enter either a title or an author's name and become dissatisfied and baffled when a request for "*Bitter Medicine* by Sarah Paretsky" yields nothing.

It is nice to be independent, but those who choose to do their own searching must be guided and counseled by trained, knowledgeable librarians. They must also be fully aware of the availability of expert assistance in the library and be encouraged to ask questions about terminology, the concept of online searching, the hardware and software operation, and particular systems, such as online or CD-ROM catalogs, INFOTRAC, WILSEARCH, EASY-NET, BOOKS IN PRINT PLUS, THE ELECTRONIC ENCYCLOPEDIA, BRS AFTER DARK, and others.

Even though computerized searching tools might be freely accessible, many patrons continue to rely on staff to do the searching for them for a variety of reasons, including the following:

- they are convinced that the librarian can do it better and faster
- they own a computer, use it for other reasons, but do not know anything about online searching
- they do not own a computer and are afraid of the unknown
- there is no time to learn about online searching
- there is no interest in learning how to do it
- they fail to understand the mechanics of computers or the online searching process
- they cannot type and having to do so slows down progress

As the use of automated systems increases, a more computer knowledgeable staff is required to use these systems and to guide and teach end-users. Library personnel must fully understand the tools and principles of online searching. Those who are not experienced in direct searching of complex systems and databases are not exempt from conducting mediated searches if they have access to systems that have the virtues of being cost-effective and easy to use. But the intelligent use of electronic tools and a staff prepared to educate end-users can only be ensured by providing personnel with a comprehensive look at computer searching and an explication of the systems and the process.

The staff development and training task is difficult because it requires continuous planning and revision as librarians come and go, technological changes occur, and system enhancements are introduced. In-house programs must be designed to encourage individual interest, cooperation, and a desire to grow professionally by continuously updating skills and developing reference expertise.

In the first place, the end-user's trainers must gain a solid understanding of the wide range of options available to libraries via a comprehensive overview of the offerings of major vendors that are of interest to academic, public, corporate, school, and special library users. The following is an example of a list of automated systems and services that might be included in an outline of the industry. It is by no means comprehensive and includes the major vendors and some well known online and CD-ROM producers.

Selected Automated Systems and Services

1. BOOKS IN PRINT PLUS:
R. R. Bowker
245 West 17th Street
New York, NY 10114
212-337-6989

BOOKS IN PRINT PLUS is a CD-ROM product that includes *Books in Print, Subject Guide to Books in Print, Forthcoming Books in Print, Supplement to Books in Print,* and *Children's Books in Print.*

It is searchable by author, title, series title, subject, publisher, key word, ISBN, price, grade, audience, year of publication, language, and more. Other features include Boolean operators, truncation, two search modes, intended respectively for novice and expert, browse mode, save searches, print and edit capability, and data formatting.

Other CD-ROM databases include:

BOOKS IN PRINT WITH BOOK REVIEWS PLUS: BOOKS IN PRINT plus unabridged book reviews from *Publishers Weekly, Library Journal, School Library Journal, Choice, Booklist, Reference and Research Book News,* and *Science Technology Book News.*

BOOKS OUT OF PRINT PLUS: Includes out-of-print and out-of-stock titles from 1979 to the present.

ULRICH'S PLUS: Regularly and irregularly published publications.

VARIETY'S COMPLETE HOME VIDEO DIRECTORY PLUS: Includes a record for every video cassette in active distribution and key facts about each release.

2. BRS:

BRS Information Technologies
1200 Route 7
Latham, NY 12110
800-345-4BRS

BRS provides access to over 135 bibliographic and full-text databases in medicine, science, technology, social science, business, humanities, and more via BRS/Search software. The databases are searchable by key words or controlled vocabulary (thesaurus descriptors); features include field qualification, Boolean operators, cross-database searching, temporary or permanent storage of searches, and more.

BRS features a user-friendly MENUS interface designed for the novice searcher. It enables one to search the system with the help of simplified menu prompts and abbreviated commands.

BRS/AFTER DARK is designed for personal computer users and

provides after-hours (6 P.M. to 4 A.M. EST, Monday through Friday, and all day Saturday and Sunday) access at reduced prices to a select group of databases—using a user-friendly interface.

BRS/COLLEAGUE is a user-friendly, menu-driven service for health professionals with minimal or no online search experience.

3. DIALOG:
DIALOG Information Services
3460 Hillview Avenue
Palo Alto, CA 94304
800-334-2564

The oldest and largest online information retrieval service presently provides access to about 300 bibliographic, full-text, directory/dictionary, and numeric databases covering all subject areas. Features include key word and controlled vocabulary searching, Boolean operators, searching by field (record segment), searching several files simultaneously (OneSearch feature), the ability to scan the indexes of a variety of files (DIALINDEX), a wide variety of practice (ONTAP, or ONline Training and Practice) databases, permanent or temporary search strategy saving function, and more.

DIALOGLINK software provides access to services via a personal computer, featuring one-step logon and the ability to keep track of online costs.

DIALOG KNOWLEDGE INDEX provides discounted online access to a selected group of databases for personal computer users during evening/night (6 P.M. to 6 A.M.) and weekend hours. It features simplified software for novice searchers.

Two menu-driven packages are available for use by those with little or no training or experience—DIALOG BUSINESS CONNECTION provides access to business and financial data and DIALOG MEDICAL CONNECTION allows easy access to information covering medicine, biology, life sciences, and related fields.

DIALOG OnDisc includes a growing number of CD-ROM products that are derived from the online databases, with the addition of a menu-driven option for ease of use. The line presently includes ERIC, MEDLINE, and NTIS—with more planned for the future—and its advantages are an annual, fixed subscription rate and no connect time or print charges. Information can be sorted before printing and results can be downloaded. It also can be used to create a search more inexpensively than some other sources and then access the same database online to obtain more current information and to expand the search by running it in other databases.

DIALOG Classroom Instruction Program is available to schools at a special rate. The program is designed to teach and demonstrate the process of online searching.

4. DISCLOSURE:

Disclosure Incorporated
5161 River Road
Bethesda, MD 20816
301-951-1300

DISCLOSURE, produced by Disclosure Incorporated, is a business and industry directory database available via a variety of vendor services. The compact disc version includes company profiles, annual and quarterly balance sheets, five-year summaries and growth rates, data on company officials, full text of the president's letter and management discussion from the annual report, ownership information, list of documents filed with the SEC, 10Ks (an annual report filed with the Securities and Exchange Commission that includes total sales figures, revenue, and operating income before taxes) and 10Qs (a quarterly report required by the Securities and Exchange Commission that must include a comparison of figures for the same period of the previous year), and more. It is updated bimonthly.

COMPACT DISCLOSURE is searchable in two modes—one, designed for novices, is a menu-driven system that requires no prior database search training; the second, for experienced users, emulates the DIALOG command language.

5. DOW JONES NEWS/RETRIEVAL:

Dow Jones News/Retrieval
P. O. Box 300
Princeton, NJ 08540
800-257-5114

DOW JONES NEWS/RETRIEVAL provides current information on financial markets, i.e., stock quotes and market averages, business and financial reports, full text of the *Wall Street Journal, Washington Post, Barron's, Standard and Poor's* company profiles, and financial data.

It features an easy-to-use menu-driven system, with the option of a command-driven system for quick access to a feature, if the name of the feature is known, i.e., //WSJ to get right to the *Wall Street Journal*; user prompts are easy to understand and helpful.

6. EASYNET:

Telebase Systems, Inc.
763 W. Lancaster Avenue
Bryn Mawr, PA 19010
215-526-2800

This is a gateway system providing access to BRS, DIALOG, NEWSNET, ORBIT, VU/TEXT, WILSONLINE, and others, potentially allowing the user to search in over 900 databases covering all subjects. Its features include a menu-driven system, one common command language, a choice of either letting the system pick the database(s) or, if the searcher is experienced, allowing the user to select, cross-database searching (in EASYNET version III), help screens, and an SOS function that brings in human assistance.

The EASYNET interface is also available through Western Union's EASYLINK—known as INFOMASTER; it is named IQUEST on COMPUSERVE and ALANET PLUS on ALANET.

EINSTEIN is a specialized version of EASYNET created for high school and undergraduate students. It provides access to ninety selected databases.

The ANSWER MACHINE, consisting of a workstation that includes a keyboard and a color monitor, with a microcomputer, modem, and printer concealed inside the unit, provides access to the more than 900 databases available via EASYNET, with either the patrons paying for use, or the library paying an annual fee for unlimited use of the databases.

7. ELECTRONIC ENCYCLOPEDIA:

Grolier Electronic Publishing
Sherman Turnpike
Danbury, CT 06816
203-797-3500

A compact laser disc (CD-ROM) version of Grolier's *Academic American Encyclopedia*, it is also available online via a number of database vendor services. It offers quick and easy access to information, such as brief facts, subject overviews, and comprehensive bibliographies. Indexed by subject, it includes tables, fact boxes, bibliographies, and cross-references.

Features include searching by key word or concepts, simplified menus and commands, Boolean logic, function keys, browse, list (of key word(s), names, or titles), various display modes, and yearly updates.

8. FACTS ON FILE NEWS DIGEST:

Facts on File Publications
460 Park Avenue South
New York, NY 10016
212-683-2244

A CD-ROM database that provides the full text and maps of news items from the 1980–1987 *News Digest* volumes, it features interactive tutorial and help screens, date limitation function, browse mode, key word and Boolean logic, truncation, cross-referencing, and zoom function to magnify a map location. Also available is a teacher's guide with lesson plans; annual update discs are included.

9. INFOTRAC:

Information Access Company
362 Lakeside Drive
Foster City, CA 94404
800-227-8431

INFOTRAC provides current bibliographic information from Information Access Company's MAGAZINE INDEX, BUSINESS INDEX, and LEGAL RESOURCE INDEX (LEGALTRAC) on video disc. INFOTRAC II, or MAGAZINE INDEX PLUS, provides access to the four most current years of the MAGAZINE INDEX, plus citations from the current three months of the *New York Times*. A special version of INFOTRAC for undergraduate research is available on CD-ROM. Enhanced INFOTRAC, including access to DIALOG ONDISC CD-ROM databases as well, is also available.

Features include color-coded function keys, easy searching (with single key stroke) of cross-references, and the ability to link up to six workstations. INFOTRAC is designed for novice searchers.

10. LEXIS/NEXIS:

Mead Data Central
9443 Springboro Pike
P. O. Box 933
Dayton, OH 45401
800-543-6862

LEXIS, designed for lawyers needing fast access to research material, includes full-text databases offering access to a wide variety of legal resources, for example, federal and state law, law material that is subject specific (banking, commerce, labor, tax, health, trade, etc.), international law, Shepard's Citations Service, and others.

The NEXIS service includes a wide variety of files located in different libraries. For example, the NEXIS library includes newspaper, magazine, newsletters, and wires files that can be searched separately, all at once (OMNI), or in specific groups, such as current (1985 or later), archival (pre-1985), general business files, finance, government, trade/technology. Other libraries include the ENCYCLOPEDIA BRITANNICA; ASAP II LIBRARY; the full-text MAGAZINE ASAP and TRADE AND INDUSTRY ASAP databases produced by the Information Access Company; CMPCOM, computers and communications; BUSABS, business abstracts, including ABI/INFORM, GOVNWS, government and political news; APOLIT, Associated Press Political Library; GENMED, general medical library, and much more.

Features include searching by segments (fields), Boolean operators, menu screens, display/print options, full-featured and powerful command language, cross-file searching, a practice library (database), and computer-assisted instruction (CAI) at reduced rates.

Access is either by MEAD dedicated terminals with very convenient function keys or, using a personal computer, via LEXIS/NEXIS Communication Software—customized for ease of use.

11. MEDLARS:
National Library of Medicine
4600 Rockville Pike
Bethesda, MD 20209
800-638-8480

Produced by the National Library of Medicine, this database provides access to biomedical literature that is international in scope. Articles from over 3,000 journals are indexed. Records include bibliographic data and abstracts. Searching is done by controlled vocabulary and key word and is also searchable by field and a variety of modifiers.

GRATEFUL MED is a front-end software program with a menu-driven interface designed for both novices and expert searchers. It features a browse or select function for subject head-

34 / Personnel Needs and Changing Reference Service

ings, has cross-references, help screens, automatic logon, searching, and disconnect from MEDLARS.

PAPERCHASE is a simplified and totally menu-driven system designed for the novice who knows little or nothing about online searching. Features include the ability to use natural language that is automatically translated into the appropriate format—retrieving a list of related subject headings and title words; uses Boolean operators "AND" and "OR" to combine sets.

12. NEWSNET:

Newsnet
945 Haverford Road
Bryn Mawr, PA 19010
800-345-1301

This is a full-text database containing over 300 newsletters, most of which are not available via any other vendor. The focus is on business and industry, i.e., telecommunications, investment, taxation, electronics, computers, aerospace, defense, banking and finance, international business, and more. NEWSNET also provides up-to-the-minute data from newswires—AP DATASTREAM, BUSINESS NEWS WIRE, PR NEWSWIRE, REUTERS, JIJI (Japan/Far East), UPI.

Designed for businesspeople/novice searchers, the system accepts natural language—key words or phrases. It features a combination menu-driven and command-driven system; search options include Boolean logic, proximity searching, truncation, string searching, modification by date or date range.

13. ORBIT:

Pergamon Orbit Infoline
8000 West Park Drive
McLean, VA 22102
800-421-7229

ORBIT offers online access to more than sixty databases in the fields of science, technology, engineering, electronics, energy, environment, chemistry, patents, trademarks, and more. Many of them are available exclusively via ORBIT and access to some require special permission from the database producer.

Command-driven, ORBIT features proximity searching, truncation, Boolean logic, and field searching.

There are three subscription choices and each includes training instructions: the first consists of a workbook with step-by-step instructions, exercises for practice, and access to selected files for three hours of practice time; the second includes a day-long training workshop that provides instruction, a workbook, hands-on practice, and one and a half hours of free practice time on certain files; the third provides on-site training that is tailor-made to meet the needs of the particular library, and free practice time.

14. PRO-SEARCH:
Personal Bibliographic Software, Inc.
412 Longshore Drive
Ann Arbor, MI 48105
313-996-1580

This front-end program provides easy access to DIALOG and BRS using menus for novices, or BRS or DIALOG command language for expert searchers.

Its features include the ability to search DIALOG using BRS commands and to search BRS using DIALOG commands, formulating and editing search strategies offline, online access to DIALOG bluesheets or BRS Aid Pages, upload searches from disks, download records for offline review, automatic logon and logoff, help screens, and much more.

PRO-CITE is formatting software for bibliographic and textual records management. There are twenty predefined or six user-defined workforms; all fields are searchable using Boolean logic. It also features truncation, full-screen editor, indexing by any field, and more.

BIBLIO-LINKS is a program that converts records downloaded from online database systems into PRO-CITE records, and it links

PRO-SEARCH online searching and bibliographic database management using PRO-CITE.

15. SCI-MATE:

Institute for Scientific Information
3501 Market Street
Philadelphia, PA 19104
800-523-4092

A gateway software package offered by the Institute for Scientific Information, this was developed for research specialists and medical professionals. It allows access to DIALOG, BRS, ORBIT, and the National Library of Medicine database (MEDLINE).

It features menus that automatically translate the search terms entered into the search languages used by the accessible vendor systems. Search strategy can be formulated offline. However, knowledge of the structure of the databases chosen to search is necessary.

SCI-MATE MANAGER allows formatting of records downloaded from databases via SCI-MATE, and features Boolean logic, truncation, and string searching.

SCI-MATE EDITOR is used for formatting bibliographic records.

MARC-MATE is a function which allows for storage and retrieval of OCLC MARC records to SCI-MATE-readable database, using editor.

16. UMI CD-ROM PRODUCTS:

University Microfilms International
300 North Zeeb Road
Ann Arbor, MI 48106
800-521-3044

Designed for fast and easy access to UMI (University Microfilms International) databases, ABI/INFORM ONDISC provides access to the five most recent years of a heavily used online business database with bimonthly updates, DISSERTATION ABSTRACTS ONDISC includes archival discs containing abstracts of doctoral dissertations and master's theses from 1861 to June 1984 and current material from July 1984 to the present with annual updates, NEWSPAPER ABSTRACTS ONDISC offers citations and abstracts of articles from the *New York Times, Wall Street Journal, Christian Science Monitor, Los Angeles Times, Chicago Tribune, Boston Globe,* and *Atlanta Constitution*. PERIODICAL ABSTRACTS ONDISC provides access to current articles (citations and abstracts) from 300 general reference periodicals including *Time, Newsweek, Psychology Today, Scientific American,* and *U.S. News & World Report*.

The databases feature a menu-driven format, help windows, tutorial, Boolean logic, proximity searching, truncation, and field searching.

17. VU/TEXT:

VU/TEXT Information Services, Inc.
325 Chestnut Street, Suite 1300
Philadelphia, PA 19017
800-323-2940

An online retrieval system that provides access to the full text of over thirty-five regional newspapers, full text of selected articles from 150 regional business journals and newspapers, business summaries from over 1500 publications (*Forbes, Wall Street Journal, New York Times,* etc.); full text of *Time, Fortune, Money, Life, Sports Illustrated,* and *People*; AP, PR NEWSWIRE, BUSINESS NEWS, and other wires.

Featuring a powerful, relatively easy to use search language, VU/TEXT is command-driven. The system includes right-hand truncation, adjacency searching, proximity searching, temporary search saves, Boolean logic, and automatic plurals (ending in "s"). Special educational packages for classroom instruction purposes are available for a flat fee.

18. WILSONLINE:

H. W. Wilson Company
950 University Avenue
Bronx, NY 10452
800-462-6060

This service offers electronic versions of the H. W. Wilson indexes, including APPLIED SCIENCE AND TECHNOLOGY INDEX, ART INDEX, CUMULATIVE BOOK INDEX, EDUCATION INDEX, LC MARC DATABASE, READERS' GUIDE TO PERIODICAL LITERATURE, and all the others. The system was designed for easy access by both inexperienced and experienced searchers and is searchable by using either controlled vocabulary or free text terms.

Features include Boolean operators, online thesaurus, qualifiers, automatic switching from "see" references to a preferred term, proximity searching, nested Boolean logic, and cross-file searching.

WILSEARCH is a front-end software package featuring a database selection menu, menu of general subject areas, a search strategy menu, an on-screen help window, as well as automatic logon and logoff from WILSONLINE. Up to ten citations can be downloaded for review and printing.

WILSONDISC, a CD-ROM system, offers the simplest and easiest access to the Wilson databases while allowing switching to either WILSEARCH or WILSONLINE.

All three access routes to the databases form a single, integrated search system. For example, WILSONDISC can be searched for retrospective data (no online charges) and then WILSEARCH or WILSONLINE can be accessed for current information.

The above descriptions of the various products and vendor systems and services are by no means complete. They are meant to be indicators of content and various means of access. This list is merely representative of what is presently available in electronic format. The variety of databases, material covered, and search protocols is staggering. Yet the knowledgeable information specialist must be aware of what is around, as well as what is to come. The first prerequisite for a good reference librarian is cognizance of the resources, and awareness of options and possibilities.

Training for the Search Process

The next step in a staff education program is to review the online searching process in general by tracing the automated information retrieval path from its beginning—the query.

I. Analysis of the query
   A. Determine the subject
   B. Determine the user's needs and objectives
   C. Relate the need to the identified subject category or categories
   D. Identify the appropriate information source, i.e., vendor service(s), CD-ROM system, full text, bibliographic, dictionary/directory, or numeric database(s)
   E. As defined by the reference interview, describe the topic of the search in detail, using a search query form
II. Formulate the search strategy
   A. Select key words or phrases to further define the topic by drawing on the user's knowledge of the subject, index terms used in sources already checked
   B. Select descriptors (thesaurus terms) from the chosen database(s) list of terms; frequently the search can be further refined by locating more precise, broader, narrower, or related terms
   C. Select modifiers, i.e., language, date range, geographic location, document type (article, research report, guide, fact summary, bibliography, etc.)
III. Conduct search
   A. Log on to system

1. Select database(s)
2. If menu-driven system, follow on-screen instructions
B. Enter terms, combine concepts using Boolean operators, enter modifiers
C. Retrieve and display results, and select records for printing
D. Define print format
E. Log off (disconnect from system)

IV. Analyze search results
A. Are retrieved data relevant, current, precise, complete?
1. If so, online search completed
2. If not, reexamine search strategy and database choices
B. Revise search strategy and/or select a different system or other database(s)
1. Limit search to specific fields
2. Expand statement to search all fields
3. "NOT" out unnecessary terms to further define relevancy
4. Narrow the search by using more precise terms
5. Rather than using just descriptors, combine them with key words
C. Repeat the search process when necessary

The search path should be explained and illustrated, using real queries for effectiveness. Once the basics are understood, a discussion and demonstration of the library's automated information retrieval systems should follow, along with an explication of the kind of equipment used to access remote databases and end-user systems, including CD-ROM products. The hardware (microcomputer or terminal, modem, printer, cables, hard-disk drive, CD-ROM drive, etc.) and the software (telecommunications and searching software, compact disc, and so forth) must be defined and shown. Hands-on experience is essential. Practice periods, perhaps using search requests received in the past, are a must, with an emphasis on the importance of preparation before going online.

Vendor videos and demonstration disks, easy to use menu-driven end-user software, CD-ROM products, and computer-based training packages can be used to supplement in-house education and training programs. They should not, however, be acquired as substitutes for the human element that is so necessary for communicating thoughts, problems with concepts, and understanding of all or part of the search process. The advantage in using these aids is to reinforce and review concepts and procedures.

Vendor training should be a requirement for all searchers once a basic understanding of the process is gained. Also, follow-up advanced sessions, as well as system updates, are valuable because they allow staff to further develop skill in the use of particular systems and databases.

If a microcomputer is used to create in-house files, it can be used to develop a deeper understanding of the process of creating a database—file structure, data entry, indexing, formatting, retrieval. The job of maintaining and using these files should result in a greater appreciation of the importance of accuracy and planning when updating information or when entering or retrieving data. Exercises might be developed to test the ability to formulate search strategies, and illustrate database features and hardware and software functions.

Informal individual and group discussions with the online search service supervisor should be held at regular (weekly or monthly) intervals to discuss newly acquired automated resources, problems, failed searches, misunderstandings of terminology and system operation, victories, user reactions (satisfaction or disappointment), system enhancements, new features, added or revised databases, documentation, techniques, advanced searching methods, shortcuts, articles read, meetings/seminars attended, and other issues.

The information presented during any staff development or training session should definitely be reinforced with printed outlines of the program contents, facts about the online databases and systems discussed, brief guides to the searching process, sample documents, sample searches, and more.

Glossary of Computer Terminology

Since some staff may not be familiar with computer terminology (or may not admit ignorance), a "computerese" glossary for easy reference is vital. The following list is by no means comprehensive, but it illustrates just what terms and definitions might be included.

abstract: A summary of the contents of a document.

adjacency: A word or symbol that indicates the position of two terms in a record, i.e., in the same field as, in the same sentence as, adjacent to.

baud rate: The rate of speed at which devices transfer information over communications lines; usually expressed in bits per second.

bit: A single digit in the binary number system, either a "0" or a "1." See K.

Boolean logic: The use of the logical operators "AND," "OR," "NOT" to show relationships between terms when developing search strategy.

byte: A unit of consecutive binary digits that is used to represent data; eight bits of data are contained in one byte of computer storage.

CD-ROM (compact disc-read only memory): Data stored on a compact disc that can be read from, but not written to; data stored on a disc that cannot be altered, but only retrieved.

command: Words or symbols entered by the user that instruct the search system to perform certain tasks or operations.

Training and Development / 43

command language: The instruction set used to search a particular system.

computer: A programmable device that can store, process, and retrieve data in a certain format.

connect time: The time spent connected to the host computer or remote terminal; the elapsed time between entering and leaving a system or database.

CRT (cathode ray tube): A video tube (somewhat like a television picture tube) that is used to show the letters or numbers typed on the keyboard as well as the data retrieved from the system or database.

cursor: A movable flashing spot or line of light that is seen on the CRT, indicating where the next character should be entered.

database: A collection of data or a bank of files in machine-readable form.

downloading: A function of a communications program that allows the online searcher to capture the data retrieved from a remote computer and store it on a disk, a tape, or in the microcomputer's memory for later printing, editing, or addition to or creation of a customized database.

end-user: The person who uses the data retrieved by searching a computer system or online database.

field: A portion of a record containing one kind of information, such as author or title.

file: A group of records or a collection of data with common relationships.

free text searching: Searching using natural language rather than thesaurus terms/controlled vocabulary; searching by key word.

front-end system: A software program designed for easy access to a particular database or service; usually features a menu-driven system or a simplified command language and designed primarily for inexperienced searchers.

function key: A specified key on a terminal or microcomputer keyboard that achieves a particular task, i.e., change database, move to the next menu, page up or down, print records.

gateway: A microcomputer software package that connects the user to two or more vendor services; usually has simplified searching features such as automatic dial-up, logon and logoff, automatic choosing of databases and downloading.

hardware: The physical, electronic, and electrical parts of a computer system; the computer, CRT, modem, printer, cables, etc.

help button: A special key on the computer keyboard that is pressed to obtain instructions on what to do next or how to perform certain steps in the online searching process; when the button is pressed, instructions or explanations appear on the screen to assist the searcher.

interface: Any hardware or software system that links computers or computer systems.

intermediary: An information specialist who does the searching for someone else; the librarian/information specialist who connects the end-user to the information.

K (kilo): 1,024 bytes of storage; a unit of eight bits.

key word: A natural language word (rather than a thesaurus term) that is used in searching because it is likely to be found in the desired records.

logoff: To end a search by disconnecting from the automated system.

logon: To start a search by connecting to the automated system.

menu: A display of a list of options requesting that the searcher select one.

modem: Acronym for MOdulator DEModulator; a device connected to a terminal or a microcomputer that converts machine readable data into signals for transmission over telephone lines to and from computers.

network: A number of communications lines that connect computers with other computers; two or more libraries that share or exchange information and other resources.

numeric database: A database that consists of records that are mostly numeric facts—statistics, financial data, tables, etc.

offline: Any activity or processing of data that is done prior to logging on or after logging off from a system.

online searching: The process of using a computer to retrieve data stored in electronic files either at remote sites or on a compact disc available on-site; connecting to a computer to search for data.

optical disc: A disc on which great quantities of data can be stored; a laser is used to read and write to the disc.

record: All the information that makes up a single document.

response time: The time that elapses between entering a search query and receiving a response from the host computer.

ROM (read only memory): A type of memory that can be read from but not written into; data/programs stored in a computer by the manufacturer.

saved search: A search statement that is stored in a computer either temporarily or permanently for future use.

search strategy: A plan devised to retrieve specific information from a database; a method of approach to retrieving information by creating search statements using terms that are logically connected.

46 / Personnel Needs and Changing Reference Service

search system: Software/programs that are used to access a database and retrieve information from it.

telecommunications network: A company or organization that provides a communications link between the terminal or microcomputer and the remote system/host computer.

terminal: An electronic device used for communicating with a host computer/remote database system; a machine used to enter and retrieve data.

thesaurus terms: Specific terms, or controlled vocabulary, used to search a database or databases sharing the same vocabulary.

truncation: A symbol used to signal the system that variant endings of a word stem are to be searched; a method of specifying a part of a word to retrieve variant forms of the word, i.e., on DIALOG, typing "librar?" would retrieve "library," "libraries," "librarian," and so on.

vendor system: A company or organization that provides computerized database search service, i.e., DIALOG, BRS, Mead Data Central, H. W. Wilson.

user-friendly: A search system that is designed for an inexperienced searcher, offering easy-to-follow menus, commands, help screens; allows the user to access the system without knowledge of the command language and ask questions using natural language.

Sample Staff Development Sessions

The following are outlines of two sequential group sessions of staff development on computer searching for fifteen new and experienced librarians who need to gain familiarity with the capabilities, procedures, and objectives of computer searching, to

Training and Development / 47

broaden their knowledge and understanding of automated information retrieval, and to prepare to conduct searches, or assist patrons in doing so, using either simplified online or CD-ROM end-user systems.

The objectives of the sessions include the following:

- to become familiar with the computer search systems and databases available in the library so that knowledge of them will be useful to staff and patrons
- to gain an overview of computer searching: hardware, software needed, the fundamentals of searching, databases available, commands, logic, analysis of search topic, and so forth
- to outline the types of requests that are appropriate for computer searching
- to gain the ability to conduct simple searches on common available systems, e.g., WILSEARCH, BRS AFTER DARK, BOOKS IN PRINT PLUS, EASYNET.

Session One: Computer Searching Defined

I. What is computer searching?
   A. The advantages
      1. comprehensiveness
      2. efficiency
      3. currency/timeliness
      4. specificity
II. What is a database?
   A. Bibliographic databases
   B. Textual databases
   C. Numeric databases
   D. Directory/dictionary databases
III. How do I get to search a database?
   A. Major database vendors
      1. DIALOG
      2. BRS

      3. LEXIS/NEXIS
      4. PERGAMON ORBIT INFOLINE
      5. H. W. Wilson Company
      6. Other Vendors
   B. What is CD-ROM?
IV. What kind of equipment is needed to access online and CD-ROM databases?
   A. Hardware
   B. Software
      1. telecommunications software
      2. searching software

    This introductory session is followed by a tour of the computer search service(s) available in the library and demonstrations of how searches are run.

    The documentation provided should include a detailed outline of the session, a glossary of terminology, a list of the vendors and databases discussed, a list of those available in the library and in cooperating libraries in the area, a map of the library indicating the location and hours of intermediary search service(s) and end-user services, along with information on procedure and policy, and the criteria for conducting a computer search.

Session Two: Introduction to Computer Searching

   I. Making the connection
      A. Telecommunications networks
      B. Logging on and logging off
  II. Planning the search
      A. Analyzing the topic
         1. concepts/key words
         2. related terms/synonyms
         3. Boolean logic: combining concepts
 III. Selecting the database
      A. Manual selection from the database catalog

B. Online selection from online index/directory of databases
   C. The results: citation formats
      1. bibliographic citation
      2. citation and abstracts
      3. full text of article
         a. Key word in context
      4. numeric data
      5. directory/dictionary data
         a. name, address, telephone number
         b. definitions and other details
IV. Examining the results: relevancy
   A. Toward more efficient searching
      1. bibliographic modifiers: date, type of material, journal, section
      2. personal name modifiers: biographical sketch, articles about a person, articles written by a person
      3. truncation
      4. searching in specific fields
   B. Downloading search results
   C. Formatting search results
   D. Printing search results
   E. Redefining the search and exploring other database possibilities

This session includes a demonstration of how computer searches are successfully run using the techniques, commands, and modifiers that were covered in the session. The group session is followed by individual practice sessions, using exercises provided. These include one-on-one instruction and guidance by an experienced computer searcher.

The documentation supplied includes an outline of the computer search procedure, a list of definitions of commands, modifiers and other search terminology and techniques, an illustrated explanation of Boolean logic, step-by-step instructions for searching the particular system(s), a list of factors that influence the success or failure of computer searches, and sample searches, including the request statements, strategy used, system/database(s) used, and some sample records. At least ten exercises with answers are provided for individual practice sessions.

Educating the End-User

Even though online searching tools were developed with the end-user (the person who actually makes use of the data retrieved) in mind, accessing traditional online systems has, for the most part, been the job of the information specialist/librarian/intermediary. This has been simply because this person possesses the knowledge and expertise to effectively use complex, expensive electronic systems that offer access to hundreds of databases by using powerful command languages and a host of special features. The growth in popularity of the personal computer, as well as an increasingly computer-literate lay population, prompted database vendors, producers, and publishers to develop products that would make it easy for anybody to enjoy the rewards of finding information quickly and painlessly by pressing a few buttons and letting the computer do the hunting.

The trend toward user independence has been further encouraged by the changes in the way data are stored and retrieved in libraries. Even the catalog (the key to the collection) is more commonly available in online or ondisc format and, presumably, easily searchable by novices with little or no understanding of the concepts of automated information retrieval. Gateways, front-ends and CD-ROM products, with their simplified command languages, menu-driven interfaces, step-by-step on-screen instructions, and help buttons are attractive alternatives to mediated searching because they offer low-cost or free searching to just about anybody with the inclination to explore the possibilities. Indeed, there is a percentage of the population that does not want to rely on librarians when it comes to getting at information by

Training and Development / 51

electronic means. They enjoy the freedom of looking for what they want when they need it; they do not like undergoing the required interviews, negotiations, or the usual wait (sometimes up to two weeks) for the results of a mediated search. This is particularly true when their need is urgent, i.e., for recent market trends or company take-over information needed by a business executive, for research on a particular drug treatment vital to a doctor, or for a bibliography concerned with studies of latchkey children needed for an undergraduate term project.

But what about the quality of do-it-yourself searching? Generally librarians will agree that user independence is good for a variety of reasons, including the following:

- It is done at the end-user's convenience.
- End-users respond positively to rapid data retrieval accomplished without having to explain to someone else what is needed.
- Searching on simplified systems, particularly CD-ROM products that offer unlimited free searching without the ticking of the connect-time clock, is economical for both the library and the user.
- The staff load at the reference desk is reduced, allowing more time for handling complex queries and completing collection maintenance tasks.

But these benefits have little bearing on satisfying results for most independent end-users. It is true that a number of studies of end-user searchers and searching conducted in academic, corporate, special, public, and school library settings have found that those people who work at achieving a good level of understanding of computerized systems and some searching skill, do achieve success working independently. But the majority of would-be end-users, in order to be really competent to help themselves, would require lessons that address the capabilities of information retrieval systems, subject analysis, search strategy development, and the operation of computer-assisted reference tools. A list of some of the characteristics of typical end-users should help clarify some of the problems experienced by many do-it-yourselfers:

- End-users do not know database content and tend to take a great deal of time rummaging around to locate information and complete a search.
- System features as well as limitations are not well understood, if they are known at all.
- End-users tend to search only the few databases that they know fairly well.
- They are generally computer-illiterate.
- The knowledge and skill necessary to search a database is poor or lacking.
- The ability to analyze what is really needed and how to get at it is lacking.
- They are unaware of printed search aids, such as manuals, quick reference guides, and thesauri. Even when they are made aware of the fact that such documentation will improve searching, some end-users reject them because they tend to make the searching process seem like work.
- Novices are ignorant of the importance of pre-search preparation and are inclined to do little or none of it.
- The ability to select appropriate terminology and search modifiers is lacking.
- Because of the belief that the computer is always correct, the data retrieved are thought to be terrific even if the data are wrong or insufficient.
- Do-it-yourselfers tend to have little or no knowledge or understanding of Boolean logic, file structure, command language, and so forth.
- They generally lack the ability to analyze search results, recognize a bad approach, or revise unsuccessful search strategy.
- Undergraduates, and public or school library users in particular, are all too frequently ignorant of bibliographic sources and have poor library and search skills.

- End-users tend to search infrequently and forget how to use particular systems.

One of the most touted features of end-user products has been ease of use. But simplicity does not extend to content, indexing, and access points, so the data stored in the variety of general and scholarly databases cannot be accessed effectively unless the searcher develops some skill in subject analysis, the use of logical connectors, and data manipulation. Since no end-user system exists that is so totally "friendly" that laypersons can just sit down and happily search and retrieve relevant data, the availability of educating, training, and counseling personnel is absolutely essential. End-user support service should be readily available at libraries as an integral part of reference work, regardless of where the microcomputer used for the searching is located—in the library, in a subject department of a university, at an executive's desk, a doctor's office, a college dormitory, at home, or anywhere else. Librarian-information specialists have a professional responsibility to assume the role of teacher/consultant by providing anyone interested in doing their own computerized searching with the knowledge and skills necessary to the successful use of electronic resources. At the same time, people must be assured that they do not have to go it alone if they do not want to. End-user searching must be presented as an *option* and not as the ultimate means to answering all information needs in full.

University, college, high school, and elementary school faculty and students, as well as corporate executives, professionals, and the general public, function in an information environment—an environment that should not be limited for them by the lack of familiarity with powerful electronic resources. Library orientation programs for users should emphasize the relevance of online databases to research, the completion of assignments, business profits, and the overall enrichment of life. Research methods courses and classroom instruction should teach basic library skills and the principles of automated information retrieval, while encouraging end-user searching.

Group sessions, sponsored by libraries, system and product vendors, associations, cooperatives, government organizations, and others, should not be one-time efforts. Rather, they should provide quick and easy lessons in the searching process, the arrangement of electronic databases, the scope and contents of the available databases and how to conduct searches, using Boolean logic, particular command languages, and other features. An abundance of examples of searches and strategies should be available for discussion, along with hand-outs. These should include sample searches, the contents of databases, a glossary of terms, a graphic illustration of Boolean logic, a list of the databases available for searching with descriptions of their contents and limitations, and informational sheets describing the library's mediated online searching service and end-user support program. These orientation sessions should be repeated as often as necessary to review the material covered and to provide updates on the various systems and services. Of course, all orientation sessions should include an opportunity for hands-on experience to stimulate interest in electronic searching and provide the encouragement to actually conduct some searches.

Small group and one-on-one teaching and counseling sessions should be available to anyone—with or without the benefit of group orientation. These must often be tailor-made to meet particular interests and levels of need. Also, before delving into the subject of automated information retrieval, the level of knowledge and competency of end-users should be determined—i.e., is the librarian talking to chemists or engineers who are technology-oriented, research faculty or graduate students who need subject-specific training, undergraduates who need quick access to general databases, or young students in need of basic skills and stimulation to learn?

These sessions work best if they last no longer than two hours. This allows ample time to introduce concepts, explain commands, menus and database contents, illustrate different types of searches, and provide some hands-on experience, especially logon and logoff procedures. The prospective end-user should then be walked through as many searches as is necessary to gain the confidence to go ahead independently.

After getting them going, librarians should assume the role of consultant, to explain and re-explain search protocol, logic statements, fields, search modification, and so forth, to teach subject specialists who utilize only a small number of specialized databases how to use others when the need arises.

Instead of conducting the pre-search and post-search interviews that are characteristic of mediated searching, the librarian as consultant works directly with end-users, counseling them in the search process and/or guiding them through a particular search. This is done by helping them to define a topic, select one or more databases, chose terms, develop a search strategy, demonstrate the use of search aids, hand-hold during the search, review the plan, revise the approach, and explain the results.

Individual instruction and small group sessions are most successful when conducted by information specialists who are encouraging, open, friendly, patient, and cooperative. This attitude attracts users who can, in the atmosphere created, gain the confidence required to talk freely about their information needs, reveal ignorance and uncertainty, and request all sorts of help without fear of being judged. Because this enhanced role of the librarian/information specialist requires a great deal of time and dedication, some professionals might question the validity of actively encouraging massive do-it-yourself searching activity.

Intermediary searching, professionally conducted by the librarian, is in no danger of being phased out. Only an expert can handle complex requests, complicated search protocols, and intricate database systems, and many people do not have the time or inclination to retrieve their own information. However, end-user searching is definitely attractive and valuable enough to be here to stay, and to increase. It is thought to be beneficial, especially to young people, in terms of motivation, because a microcomputer is used—and it is fun. It will become increasingly popular as the population gains a deeper knowledge of and more experience with automated information retrieval concepts and techniques. Various studies have found that presently only a small percentage of laypersons trained to search actually do so, or do it irregularly. But the teaching/training/counseling effort is not in vain. By gaining an understanding of the benefits and advantages of computerized systems and the power of electronic tools, people tend to become more intelligent users of all library resources and mediated search services as well.

3
Case Studies

Twenty-five case studies are presented below to demonstrate a variety of approaches to research, the different methods used to determine the true need, as opposed to perceived/stated need, and the choices made to connect people with information. Each study shows that the selection of sources and the use of the resources of other libraries (by direct referral, networks, or cooperative systems) is dependent upon staff knowledge and skill, attention to individual requests, a lively interest in the reference process, and the ability to think.

All of the questions and the circumstances presented here are real. Some have been selected from personal files, while others are based on the experiences of colleagues who work in different types of libraries. No effort was made to emphasize the use of public libraries, but in many cases the patron's tale was told to a public librarian—the human source of last resort in the information hunt.

Online databases were frequently used to locate information or to supplement the material retrieved manually. It is not at all unusual that in these examples Mead Data Central (NEXIS) and DIALOG were used more than any other vendor system. Martha Williams's study of the online industry reveals that these two vendors together have achieved the highest use rate and the greatest percentage of revenue.

This exploration of techniques employed by personnel in different types of libraries illustrates what it takes to expand reference work in order to provide quality service. The case studies can be used as teaching aids, and to test staff knowledge of library

58 / Personnel Needs and Changing Reference Services

resources, reference skills, and the ability to blend manual and automated information retrieval systems.

1. *My husband had a slight cut on his hand that led to severe infection and hospitalization. He was diagnosed as having cellulitis. I need a nontechnical definition of the condition and information about treatment.*

This question was asked of the science librarian in a large urban public library. The patron said she had checked some medical reference books but did not find much. What had she looked at? Only the brief technical definitions in *Blakiston's Gould Medical Dictionary, Stedman's Medical Dictionary,* and *Taber's Cyclopedic Medical Dictionary* had been examined.

The librarian went to the shelves with the patron to look at the medicine and health encyclopedias and guides written for the layperson. Again, only brief descriptions of the disease were found, but an indication of the cause, "when bacteria infect deeper levels of the skin," and the treatment, "quick treatment with penicillin and erythromycin," were clearly stated in the *Columbia University College of Physicians and Surgeons Complete Home Medical Guide.*

The reason for the doctor's haste in hospitalizing her husband was also found—the entry states that the disease can spread quickly throughout the body, via the lymph nodes, making a delay in treatment potentially fatal.

Since the patron indicated that she was interested in recent studies and reports on the treatment of cellulitis, she was referred to the online search service, where a new reference interview took place. The decision was made to check the MAGAZINE INDEX and COMPREHENSIVE CORE MEDICAL LIBRARY (a full text database) using BRS. The patron rejected the idea of searching MEDLINE because she did not have the time to find the specialized journals. The MAGAZINE INDEX did not contain the term "cellulitis." CCML was searched next, using the search statement: "cellulitis same hand same treatment$." ("$" is the symbol used in BRS for truncating a word so that the search would include the plural.) The patron asked if she could have the text of the articles that looked particularly interesting to her, e.g., Roger Finch, "Infection Today: Skin and Soft-Tissue Infections," *Lancet*, 23 January 1988, 164–68. The librarian furnished them while online.

The patron was pleased that she had quickly increased her knowledge of cellulitis and remarked that she felt she could cope with her husband's condition better now that she understood it.

2. *I need information on the Democratic candidates' campaign positions on day care for a class debate. I'm assigned to take the position of a Democrat.*

The student asked this question of the librarian in her community college library prior to Super Tuesday, 1988. Since recent material was required, the student was referred to the *New York Times Index* and *Reader's Guide to Periodical Literature.* Nothing really recent (within the last three to four months) was found.

The next suggestion was to examine recent newspapers and news magazines to look for relevant articles. The student did this for about an hour and returned to the reference desk without finding anything of substance. She was becoming frustrated and anxious about the debate, scheduled for the next day, and stated her concern to the librarian: "What do I do now? There must be some way to find something more!"

An online search service was available at the city's public library and a telephone call confirmed that the student could request an online search either in person or over the telephone. In order to save time while satisfying the urgent need for information, the student discussed her needs over the telephone.

The NEXIS APOLIT (Associated Press Political Service) file was chosen by the online search specialist because it contains data on election campaigns, political issues, and candidates' positions. By combining the terms "Democratic campaign" and "day care," the librarian retrieved a number of recent stories, i.e., *Washington Post*, March 14, 1988, F71+; *Christian Science Monitor*, March 3,

1988, 13 +; a March 6, 1988 Associated Press Political Service story containing excerpts from the political speeches delivered by the candidates.

The student arrived at the public library after class (as arranged) and the information specialist searcher discussed the material retrieved for her. She left with recent, full-text data on the candidates' positions, background information on the day care issue, and quotations from position statements—certainly enough material for a debate!

3. *What is the name for a group of crocodiles?*

The patron told a branch librarian (of an urban public library system) that he had checked dictionaries, encyclopedias of reptiles, and encyclopedias of mammals—but to no avail. He had looked up a variety of animals in books on mammals and had found some names—a litter of dogs, a pride of lions—but nothing for a group of crocodiles. A number of other sources were examined, including unabridged dictionaries, word and phrase books, and general encyclopedias, but the search was fruitless. The patron was then referred to the main library's science department, but again, nothing was found. The next stop was the general reference desk. This referral yielded the first promising clue. The index to *The Book of Lists* (1977) showed an entry for "Animals: names for groups of." On page 135 a list of "25 Wonderful Collective Nouns for Animals" was found, but there was no name for a group of crocodiles and no source given for the list other than the editors.

The librarian, commenting that the question was really intriguing, asked the patron if he wanted the search to continue. Without much hope for success, he agreed and left his name and telephone number.

On the following morning the reference librarian called his telephone reference service colleague to find out if her file of difficult questions contained anything on the subject. Fortunately, it did! Under "Animals, Groups of" a source entitled, *An Exal-*

tation of Larks (unexpectedly classed in 427) was found. The book is a beautifully illustrated and fascinating collection of documented and verified group names. The introduction traces the origins of such group names back to about 1450 and the *Egerton Manuscript*. The author considers *The Book of St. Albans* (1486) to be the most complete and important of the early lists.

Since there is no index to this wonderful source, one is forced to read the entire book—not an unpleasant job. On page 93, a reference to another list in C. E. Hare, *Language of Field Sports*, includes the name for a group of crocodiles—"a bask of crocodiles."

The telephone reference librarian contacted the patron and gave him the information and the source. He was surprised, fascinated, and wished to see the book. A copy was retrieved from the language department collection and held at the reference desk until he was able to come to the library later in the day.

4. *What is the Baudot code and where can I get a copy of it?*

Early one evening a student assistant working in a college library was approached by a freshman (and devout computer hacker) who was filled with enthusiasm about his latest projects. He volunteered all sorts of information about his computer system, modem, subscription to COMPUSERVE, and programming problems. He babbled on about a communications network he was having problems gaining access to. He said that he had even called the person in charge of the system and found out that his problem is caused by the fact that he needs to use the Baudot code—and no, the company could not send him a copy of it.

The student assistant did not know what the hacker was talking about but, using the word "computer" as a clue, suggested that a computer dictionary be checked, and pointed to the appropriate shelves. In Weik, Martin H., *Standard Dictionary of Computers and Information Processing*, he discovered that the Baudot code is a binary code "that uses five binary digits to represent a character. . . . The code is also designated as the Standard Teletypewriter code."

He returned to the reference desk with a photocopy of this definition and asked where he should go next. The student assistant read the definition of the code and guessed it might be found in a book on electronics in the university's engineering library.

The hacker ran out of the building and to the engineering library to retell his story, omitting no details. The librarian-intern at the science desk (upon hearing "Baudot code") reached for Buchsbaum, Walter H., *Buchsbaum's Complete Handbook of Practical Electronic Reference Data,* located a reference to the Baudot code on page 343, with Figure 14-7 on the next page entitled, "Baudot 5-bit code," and showed it to the excited patron. He looked at it, expressed his pleasure with the service and headed, once again, to the copy machine.

5. *My assignment is to write a paper on criticism of the modern Olympics and to give a summary of the history of the Olympic Games.*

The student checked the high school library catalog, but found only one book on the shelves. He then searched INFOTRAC, a CD-ROM index to periodical literature, and retrieved citations to some significant articles. He located some of the articles and returned to the librarian, because he thought that he did not have enough background material or recent information on criticism of the games, especially the 1988 Winter and Summer Olympics.

Since the high school library collection was exhausted, the student was referred to the public library's main library where free online database searching is available. Armed with a note from the school (in case high school students did not qualify for the service), the youngster approached the reference desk. He showed the librarian the note, the book, and the article references he had and stated his problem, along with the solution he hoped for.

A search was run in the NATIONAL NEWSPAPER INDEX, the MAGAZINE INDEX and NEWSEARCH (current month from both databases) and a bibliography of current citations was printed out. The student was shown how to interpret the citations and was sent to the periodical room to retrieve them. He then followed another suggestion and checked the catalog for titles on the Olympics. He was also referred to the young adult librarian for more background material located in a pamphlet file.

6. *How can I find articles and reports on the geology of the Catskill Mountains in New York?*

A lunchtime visit to the public library in the small city where the patron was employed turned up very little in print. On the way home that day he visited his rather remote suburban public library. The only resources available were general encyclopedias and descriptive material for travelers. The librarian told him that the best route to the information would be via a subject request sent to the regional library.

The request was processed and quickly arrived at the desk of the regional library's online search specialist. Using DIALOG, GEOREF (American Geological Institute) was searched, combining the terms "Catskill?" ("?" is the symbol for truncation, to include the plural in the search) and "geology" and "New York State." Some appropriate citations were selected and printed and mailed to the patron, along with instructions to request copies of the articles and reports he was interested in obtaining at his local library. The information retrieved included the following:

> "Trip I: The Catskills Revisited," Constance Manos and Russell H. Waines, State University of New York at New Paltz, Department of Geological Science Field Trip Guidebook, Annual Meeting of the New York State Geological Association, 1987.

> "Exposures of the Hudson Valley Fold-Thrust Belt, West of Catskill, New York," S. Marshak and T. Engelder, Centennial Field Guide, Northeastern Section of the Geological Society of America, Boston College, Department of Geology and Geophysics, Chestnut Hill, Mass., 1987.

64 / Personnel Needs and Changing Reference Services

"Late Wisconsinan Stratigraphy of the Catskill Mountains," D. H. Cadwell, New York State Geological Survey, Albany, New York. Bulletin–New York State Museum, 1986.

Since the sources chosen were rather specialized, a request for copies was sent to the state university library, a member library of a regional cooperative system. They were routed back to the requesting library, the patron was contacted, and he picked up the information on his way home from work.

7. *Are there current data available on the link between AIDS and tuberculosis?*

An article from the *Wall Street Journal,* entitled "Tuberculosis Rise Among AIDS Patients Raises Concern About Wider TB Infection," had been clipped from the March 13, 1986 newspaper, page 27. The patron asked if any more recent articles in newspapers and magazines were available. She also needed recent reports on the subject from medical journals. The reference librarian at the community library advised her to visit the cooperative library system's regional library because of its larger collection and online search service.

The patron showed the regional library's reference librarian/online searcher the clipping she had. She repeated her request, adding that she hoped she could get the information quickly because she had traveled a long distance and taken a day off from work to do so. She was happy to learn that an instant bibliography could be produced while she waited.

The MAGAZINE INDEX, NATIONAL NEWSPAPER INDEX and NEWSEARCH were searched via DIALOG, using the terms "AIDS" and "tuberculosis" within the same field. A number of relevant items were retrieved, including:

"Increase in Tuberculosis Tied to Spread of AIDS," *New York Times,* January 3, 1988, 12.

"The Tuberculosis-AIDS Link, After Years of Declining Slightly,

TB Rates Show Increase Correlating with AIDS Cases," *Washington Post,* August 18, 1987, WH7.

"Cases of Tuberculosis Rise, Possible Tie to AIDS is Cited," *New York Times,* May 1, 1987, A18.

"Will AIDS Make the Black Death Look Pale?" *Discover,* April 1987, 4.

The librarian then searched MEDLINE, using the same strategy, and modifying the search by language (LA = English) as well as by year of publication (PY = 1988 and PY = 1987). A number of reports on the AIDS and tuberculosis link were retrieved from such journals as *Chest, Journal of Clinical Pathology,* and the *New York State Journal of Medicine.* This last report was of particular interest to the patron because it discussed guidelines for management of tuberculosis in patients with HIV infections.

Additional information was found in such specialized sources as *American Journal of Medicine, American Review of Respiratory Disease, American Heart Journal,* and *British Medical Journal.*

"But where do I find these sources?"

The patron was directed to the periodicals room to retrieve the articles from the general interest periodicals and newspapers. However, the specialized medical journals were not held by the regional library. The patron did not have the time to wait for an interlibrary loan to be processed, so she was very happy with the librarian's referral to a medical society library, located across town, to obtain photocopies of whatever she could get.

"Are you sure that they have the articles I need? I don't want to make the trip for nothing!"

The reference librarian telephoned the medical society library, a member of the regional cooperative and open to public use, and was told that most of the material is available. She was also happy to learn that they were open late that evening so that she did not have to rush over to gather the material.

8. *Is anyone using either "heart smart" or "heartsmart" as a trademark?*

An entrepreneur, with an interest in the medical field, visited his small local library to conduct his own research. He was referred to the *Trade Names Dictionary,* 6th edition, 1988, and the *Supplement to the 6th Edition,* 1988. He found no entries for "heart smart"—spelled either as two words or one. Since the collection was inadequate for the patron's needs, the librarian suggested that he go to the main library (of the urban system) to use the *Official Gazette of the United States Patent and Trademark Office.* The patron was overwhelmed by this weekly publication, with its various indexes and number codes, and did not feel that he could use it competently. He realized that he would not be able to do a comprehensive search by himself, and if he attempted to do so, he would have to devote hours, weeks, and probably months to examine years of records!

So, the independent researcher decided that it was time for some dependence and went to the desk to ask the documents librarian for guidance. He told the patron about two databases that could do the job very quickly—TRADEMARKSCAN - FEDERAL (trademarks used on every type of product or service commercially marketed in the United States) and TRADEMARKSCAN - STATE (trademarks used on every type of product or service commercially marketed in the United States and Puerto Rico, according to information obtained from the secretaries of state of each state and Puerto Rico).

"Great! Where do I go?"

"Would you like to do your own computer search? A librarian is available to help you."

The patron responded with a firm and fearful "No!" He was then referred to the online search service, with access to DIALOG, located in the general reference room.

"Will it cost anything?"

Ready reference searches are free, and the documents librarian was sure this search would not take five minutes. In order to save both the patron's and the searcher's time, the documents librarian wrote the database names and the request statement on a search strategy form. The entrepreneur handed the form to the online search specialist, explained why he was looking for the information, and exclaimed, "If you don't find anything, I'll be rewarded!"

The librarian logged on to DIALOG. Three occurrences of "heart smart" were located in the federal record of registered trademarks: a Lever Brothers vegetable oil spread; a term used in advertising by the Washington State Beef Commission; and a health program for the prevention of heart disease sponsored by the Henry Ford Hospital in Michigan. However, no occurrences of "heartsmart" as one word were found.

Moving on to TRADEMARKSCAN - STATE, three records were found for the term as two words, and all three were for the Henry Ford Hospital in Michigan. "Heartsmart" as one word was used for paper goods and printed matter by an individual in Ohio. The entrepreneur was encouraged by the findings and remarked hopefully, "Perhaps the business in Ohio is defunct!"

9. *I have to do a report on the Cuban missile crisis. My friend has to do something on World War II and my other friend has to do the Korean War.*

Three young students, known underachievers, entered their junior high school library. With little enthusiasm for their assignments, they began to browse the book shelves and flip through the pages of various encyclopedia volumes. The librarian asked the boys what they were looking for and was bombarded with all sorts of complaints about their assignments. They said they did not like history because it is dull. They also remarked that it is hard to remember all sorts of facts and dates about "stuff" that happened long ago. Clearly, their interest and imaginations had to be stimulated. The librarian suggested that they follow her to the new ELECTRONIC ENCYCLOPEDIA, the Grolier *Academic American Encyclopedia* on CD-ROM. The sight of a computer immediately aroused the students' curiosity and their grumbling ceased.

After a demonstration of how the system works (by following the program's prompt commands), one of the students eagerly sat down and typed in "Cuban missile crisis," browsing by article title. He then pressed the key that calls up the full text of the article and discovered that the crisis occurred in October 1962, after reports that the U.S.S.R. was constructing launching sites for missiles in Cuba. Rather than invade Cuba, President John F. Kennedy "declared a 'quarantine', or naval blockade." The youngster then wanted to know if he could find more on the subject. He was instructed to increase the list of choices by conducting a word search for the words "Cuban," "missile," and "crisis."

Fifteen articles were retrieved. The first one, entitled "Blockade," was viewed because the youngster was looking for a definition of the concept: "A pacific blockade is one used in time of peace to coerce a country into fulfilling some agreement or obligation.... During the CUBAN MISSILE CRISIS of 1962, the United States established a blockade to prevent Soviet vessels from carrying missiles to Cuba." He thought he would improve his report if he added some information about President Kennedy and retrieved the article on John F. Kennedy and printed the paragraph pertaining to his handling of the missile crisis.

The student reluctantly gave his seat to one of his friends and expressed his desire to watch him find something on World War II.

The second boy did not know much about the war except that "it was big!" He had tried to focus on some aspect of the war but had found the article in the printed and bound encyclopedia long and boring. The boy was anxious to see if the computer would make his exploration of the possibilities less tedious. The first item he retrieved was a brief summary that supplied the dates the war began and ended, the cause, and the countries involved. He then scanned an article outline and quickly decided to write his report on the war in the Pacific. The librarian suggested that he narrow his topic even further and asked him to reexamine the article outline. The student finally selected Japan because he remembered his grandfather's stories about fighting there—"and they didn't have jet airplanes!" The third boy wanted his chance, so the pertinent information on the Japanese involvement in the war was quickly located and printed.

The students changed places and the third boy confidently began typing in terms and selected the proper functions with ease—he had benefited by watching his friends. He located and printed information on the background of the Korean War, the invasion of South Korea and the outcome of the war.

The boys noticed that President Harry Truman and General Douglas MacArthur were mentioned in articles on both World War II and the Korean War and they wanted to know more about the relationship between the two men. The librarian instructed them to search both names together. They chose to search the word(s) "Harry.Truman" along with "Douglas.MacArthur" (the period between the names serves as a replacement for an unknown middle name or initial). Only two articles with both names occurring in the same paragraph were found: 1. "Bradley, Omar N." and 2. "Korean War."

"Who is Bradley?" The students soon found out that Bradley was a great general in World War II and, as Joint Chiefs of Staff chairman, "supported President Harry Truman in relieving Douglas MacArthur as supreme Allied commander in Korea." In the article on Korea, the boys discovered that General MacArthur, the American commander in East Asia, was ordered to "commit his ground, air and naval forces against the North Koreans."

But why isn't there more on the two men? The librarian pointed out that by changing the search strategy to Truman and MacArthur mentioned together in an article would reveal better results. Subsequently, they retrieved seven pertinent articles: 1. "Bradley, Omar N." (again), 2. "Eisenhower, Dwight D.," 3. "Korean War" (again), 4. "MacArthur, Douglas," 5. "Truman, Harry S.," 6. "United States, History of the," 7. "World War II."

The students decided that they wanted to know more about

70 / Personnel Needs and Changing Reference Services

General MacArthur and read the text of the article devoted to him. Since it included information on his role in World War II and in the Korean War, the entire article was printed and shared by the two boys. They also looked at the other articles and printed some significant paragraphs.

The students were fascinated by the power of the "computerized" encyclopedia and asked the librarian if they would be able to get a list of baseball's most valuable players. Since they had done so well with their report research, the librarian felt it was time for a little educational fun. She asked the boys to think of the terms they would use. They quickly decided on "baseball" along with "most valuable player." What type of material is needed? Surely not article text, bibliographies, article titles, or fact boxes? The boys decided that the "tables" option would be appropriate because they were looking for a comprehensive list of players and the years they were named most valuable. To their delight, the data were quickly retrieved.

While the three were happily exploring, another student walked over to the group to ask the librarian if she could help her find something on "Momar Kadaffi." She had been unsuccessful in her search of hard copy sources. The three ELECTRONIC ENCYCLOPEDIA enthusiasts invited her to have a seat and showed her how to use it. She typed in "Kadaffi" and again found nothing. Why? Is the name spelled correctly?

The librarian then discussed another feature of computerized searching—truncation, or the ability to search for a part of a word when you are not sure of the spelling. All agreed that the name probably begins with "KADA" and this was typed, using the "word search" function. A word index came on the screen and included:

KACUR
KAD
KADANS
KADAR

KADAZANS
KADDAFI
KADDISH
KADENSHO
KADER

"A-ha! It is 'Kaddafi!' "

A word search revealed two occurrences under "Kaddafi, Muammar al-" and one under "Qaddafi, Muammar al-." Both "Kaddafi" entries were merely "see" references to "Qaddafi." The article text provided the youngster with the biographical information she needed. She then asked if she could retrieve something on the history of Libya. The three boys urged her to continue her searching. She quickly located material on the history of Libya and left the trio in order to search for periodical articles on her topics.

The three boys went on to check the catalog to locate some books mentioned in the bibliographies found at the end of the articles they retrieved from the ELECTRONIC ENCYCLOPEDIA. They left the library filled with enthusiasm and a lively interest in their topics. History had come alive and research had become fun!

10. *I need a breakdown of the voting trends on Super Tuesday, March 8, 1988.*

An executive asked her secretary to locate the report of the *New York Times*-CBS News poll taken on March 8. She assumed that it had been printed in the newspaper on March 9, but she no longer had a copy of that paper. She called the corporate librarian and asked her to locate the information in the March 9 newspaper. After a thorough search, the librarian concluded that the wrong date was given and she began to check earlier papers for clues. Because other questions had to be answered, she called the public library's telephone reference service and explained her problem and the need for a fast solution. The public librarian assured her that he would conduct an online search as soon as possible and call her back.

Since the telephone reference service has access to NEXIS, a quick answer was ensured. The *New York Times* full-text file (NYT) in the PAPERS library was searched, transmitting the terms "Super Tuesday" and "CBS w/2 (within two words of) poll" and "date aft (after) 3/8/1988." The results of the poll were published on March 10, Section A, Page 26, "After Super Tuesday, the *New York Times*/CBS News Poll, Portrait of the Super Tuesday Electorate." The results included figures for Republicans Bush, Dole, and Robertson and then for the Democrats Dukakis, Gephardt, Gore, and Jackson. The analysis gave percentages by sex, ethnic origin, age, religion, income, and was based on questionnaires completed by voters as they exited polling places in fourteen states.

The full text of the article was printed and the corporate librarian was called within fifteen minutes. A messenger was sent to pick up the print-out for the executive.

11. *What is the correct name of a religious sect referred to as the "Nubian-Islamic Hebrews" and where are its headquarters?*

A librarian working in a magazine publisher's library was asked to locate this information for one of the feature writers. He thought the best and quickest approach would be an online search and logged on to DIALOG to search MAGAZINE INDEX, NATIONAL NEWSPAPER INDEX, and RELIGION INDEX. The search was fruitless. The general encyclopedias were of no help so he reached a dead end. His next thought was to call a friend, a college librarian who seemed to have a talent for locating obscure information. The friend took the challenge and was confident he would locate the answer quickly. The secret of his success was his happy competition with a public librarian working in the reference department of an urban library; he bet her she could not find the information before he did.

The "Religious Organizations and Institutions Index" in *The Encyclopedia of American Religions* contains an entry for "Nubian

Islaamic Hebrew Mission." The group listed under entry 1158 is the Ansaaru Allah Community, or Nubian Islaamic Hebrew Mission, located at 716 Bushwick Avenue, Brooklyn, NY 11221. The information given includes the origins and beliefs of the community, its symbol, periodicals published, and sources for further information.

The data were relayed back to the magazine library and the public librarian won a dinner.

12. *I am looking for an article by Everstine or Everstein in* AmP—*whatever that is!*

A medical student, frustrated because he had written down an incomplete reference to an article he needed, asked for help at the university medical library's reference desk. When queried further, the student revealed that the article had something to do with ethics and was probably written between 1980 and 1986.

The librarian knew that *AmP* stood for *American Psychologist* and chose to do a ready reference search on DIALOG, in PSYCINFO, the most likely database to use.

The first step was to determine the correct spelling of the author's name. The search terms were entered: "AU (author) = EVERSTINE,? or EVERSTEIN,?" A journal modification was typed in: "JN = AMERICAN PSYCHOLOGIST." One article, the one the student needed, was retrieved: Everstine, Louis, et. al., "Privacy and Confidentiality in Psychotherapy," *American Psychologist*, 35 (September 1980), 828–40.

Frustration ended, the student located the hard copy journal and photocopied the article.

13. *I have to draw a picture of a famous building in Washington, D.C., and write a report on it. My school does not have a library.*

A fifth-grade student went to a small branch library in his neighborhood to complete his assignment. He browsed through the article in the *World Book Encyclopedia,* paying particular attention to the pictures. Those that were large enough to copy were of places already chosen by his classmates, so he asked the librarian for help.

In her conversation with the boy, the librarian learned that he had visited Washington during the previous summer.

"Of the buildings you visited, which did you like best?"

The youngster liked the "big museum" (Smithsonian Institution, but his friend had chosen it), the Washington Monument, the White House, and the Lincoln Memorial. "But everybody else is doing those!"

When asked if he could think of any other places he saw, he remembered going into the "giant" library with his father. "Hey! I could do that!" The boy went back to the encyclopedia and located information about the Library of Congress. But he had a new problem—the library is made up of three buildings and the pictures were too small to copy or trace.

The librarian asked him which of the three buildings looked most interesting. The youngster quickly chose the main building, opened in 1897. The search for a suitable picture was fruitless, so the librarian showed the student how to check the system's CD-ROM catalog for books on the history of the Library of Congress, thinking that they might contain illustrations. Two titles in the adult collection looked promising: Gurney, Gene, *The Library of Congress: A Picture Story of the World's Largest Library,* and Goodrum, Charles A., *The Library of Congress.*

The librarian called the main library to find out if the books were available and if they contained pictures of the main building that the child could use. An illustration of the main building and a diagram of the location of the Library of Congress on Capitol Hill was included in the first book mentioned, while the second title did not contain any pictures. The Gurney book was then held at the desk until the evening, when the child's father was able to drive to the library to borrow it with his adult card.

The youngster found the picture he needed and decided to draw the main building and the diagram so that he could show where the building is located. He also found more information on the history of the Library of Congress that he could add to his report.

14. *I want a LISA search for information on circulation systems that are IBM-compatible.*

A demanding librarian told the online search specialist, employed by the same urban/suburban library system, that he had to have a search on the LISA (Library Information Science Abstracts) database completed as soon as possible because he had a time limitation for finishing a grant proposal. He added that he had no time to "fool around with the machine" himself.

The online search specialist asked if he needed a list of products and company names or if he required reports and studies of circulation systems. The requesting librarian said he needed names and addresses and indicated that he "did some research" and wanted only a LISA search. He asked the search specialist to call him when the print-out was ready.

Acceding to the librarian's wishes, LISA was searched. Combining the terms "circulation control/de" (as a descriptor or thesaurus term) and "IBM," twenty-two records were retrieved, and included studies of particular systems and product reviews. The most recent record was dated 1983. Although probably not useful, the data were printed out for the librarian.

The searcher then proceeded to retrieve the information really needed by accessing the appropriate database—MICROCOMPUTER SOFTWARE AND HARDWARE GUIDE, updated to the current month. The search statement was typed in: "circulation and (library or libraries) and HA (compatible hardware) = IBM"

A list of seventeen circulation software packages, compatible with IBM microcomputers, was retrieved. Each record included the name of the package, release date, compatible hardware, language, required memory, price, documentation information, publisher's name/address/telephone number, descriptive annotation, and more.

The librarian was then notified that the search had been completed and the results were explained. He confessed that he really did not know anything about the contents of the LISA database and assumed that it would contain the information he needed. He admitted that the database chosen by the online search specialist provided the current information he urgently needed.

15. *Why is it blue for boys and pink for girls?*

This question was asked of a librarian in a branch of a large urban library system. The patron said that the question just came to her; she had never really thought about it before. She had been in the library earlier that day to check the etiquette books but found nothing. The question nagged at her so she decided to ask.

Assuming that the colors are symbolic of something, the librarian and the patron checked the books of symbols. Steven Olderr, *Symbolism: A Comprehensive Dictionary,* indicated that pink symbolizes (among other things!) sensuality, the flesh, femininity, effeminacy, homosexuality, joy, and good health; blue stands for truth, eternity, sorrow, the spirit of man, peace, and so forth.

The next title, *Dictionary of Mythology, Folklore and Symbols,* was somewhat frustrating. On page 228, under "blue," it says that "Merchants have designated blue to signify the birth of a boy." What about pink?" On page 1274, it reads that pink is the "color" signifying the birth of a girl.

"Is that it? Merchants decided it?"

Neither the patron nor the librarian was satisfied, but the collection yielded no other information.

The patron wanted to give up but the librarian encouraged her to wait until the main library was contacted to find out if that collection would yield an answer. The reference librarian who received the call knew exactly where to look, since the question had been asked before. An old and unique book entitled *How Did It Begin?* by R. Brasch explained it on pages 22–23: "From the days of antiquity it was believed that evil spirits hovered menacingly over the nursery. . . . It was considered that the association of blue with the heavenly sky rendered satanic forces powerless and drove them away.... Thus, the display of blue on a young child was . . . a necessary precaution."

But why blue for boys only? Girls were considered inferior to boys so the evil spirits had no interest in them. The color pink might have been given to girls later on in history because it was realized that girls had been neglected and needed a color of their own. Another explanation is given. According to European legend, "boys are found under cabbages whose colour—on the Continent of Europe—was mostly blue. Baby girls, on the other hand, were born inside a pink rose."

Both patron and librarian requested copies of this explanation. Two photocopies were sent to the branch by inter-library mail, whereupon the branch librarian mailed one of the copies to the grateful patron.

16. *What is the difference between bereavement after death by homicide and bereavement after death by illness or accident?*

A doctor requested this information at her hospital library. The material was needed quickly and the doctor had no time to do her own research. MEDLINE was the only online system available in this small library. The librarian ran the search but retrieved nothing—which was expected. She then called the medical society library, but the hospital library had no budget to pay the fee charged for the search. The doctor could not be reached to find out if she would be willing to pay. The medical library's librarian suggested contacting the public library in the nearby city because patrons were not charged fees for online searches.

The public library's information specialist was able to run the search immediately, choosing the PSYCHINFO database on DIALOG. The thesaurus was consulted and terms were selected: "grief (bereavement)," "homicide," "accidents," "disorders (illness)."

Twelve citations were retrieved by combining "grief/de (descriptor)" and "homicide/de (descriptor)" within the same field. For example:

> Kathleen V. Cowles, "Personal World Expansion: Experiences of Survivors of Murder Victims," *Dissertation Abstracts International*, 1986.
>
> Edward K. Rynearson, "Psychological Effects of Unnatural Dying on Bereavement," *Psychiatric Annals*, (May 16, 1986): 272–75.

By combining the terms "grief/de (descriptor)" and "disorders/de (descriptor)" in the same field (F), a number of relevant article references were found:

> George H. Pollock, "Childhood Sibling Loss: A Family Tragedy," *Institute for Psychoanalysis*, (May 16, 1986): 309–14.
>
> Sandra J. Klein and William Fletcher, "Gay Grief: An Examination of its Uniqueness Brought to Light by the AIDS Crisis," *Journal of Psychological Oncology*, 4, 1986, 15–25.
>
> John S. Stephenson and Dianne Murphy, "Existential Grief: The Special Case of the Chronically Ill and Disabled," *Death Studies*, 10, 1986, 135–45.

The librarian decided to try a search using "grief/de (descriptor)" and "illness (key word)." More relevant material was located.

> Anne Katterhagen, "Care for Families: Expanding Hospice Treatment Programs," *Generations*, 11, 1986–87, 39–41.
>
> Mary A. Jansen, "Psychotherapy and Grieving: A Clinical Approach," *Psychotherapy Patient*, 2, 1985, 15–25.

The hospital librarian was informed of the results later that day and was also told that they could be mailed to the hospital library. The doctor, however, did not want to wait for the post office to do the job and sent her secretary to the public library to pick up the results.

Meanwhile, the doctor added a search request for a list of books she might recommend to patients. BOOKS IN PRINT was searched on DIALOG and a bibliography was printed.

The doctor was so pleased with the service, and the cooperation between libraries, that she sent a generous donation to the public library.

17. *What is positive about Austria?*

The librarian at the reference desk of a large urban public library's main library asked the patron what she meant by "positive." She responded by saying, "Things that are good about the country!" The librarian asked her if she had the cultural history of Austria in mind. The answer was, "Positive things about life in Austria!"

Taking a new approach, the librarian asked the patron what she considered negative about the country. She answered, "It seems all you hear about is Hitler and Waldheim. There must be something positive!"

The article on Austria in the *Encyclopedia Americana* was located and the librarian scanned it with the patron in an effort to make her focus on such "positive" things as music, art, literature, the Austrian Alps, and so forth. Success at last! But her request for books on the subject was qualified by a strong statement of her fear of "those machines"—the CD-ROM catalog, so the librarian searched the catalog for her (the patron remained by the reference desk, so great was her fear). Citations and holdings information for a number of books on Austrian history and culture were selected and printed. A few travel books were also chosen because they highlighted the "positive"—places worth visiting.

The patron was then referred to the history, travel, and literature departments of the library. At each desk she repeated her desire for only the most recent titles; she did not like to read "old" books.

The patron then returned to the reference desk and told the librarian that she would also like to know what is currently being said in the newspapers and magazines that is "positive." Turning to the microcomputer, the librarian logged on to DIALOG to search NATIONAL NEWSPAPER INDEX, MAGAZINE INDEX, and NEWSEARCH (indexes the latest month for both databases) for recent articles on Austria, excluding politics and Waldheim. A number of article citations were retrieved and one (not too recent—1985) was of particular interest to her: Paul Hofmann, "The Capital from A to Z: Vienna is a Place of Coffeehouse Culture, Abundant Music and an Occasionally Blue Danube," *New York Times,* 134, Section 10 (Travel Section), August 25, 1985, 114.

The patron's comments on her love of Viennese music gave the librarian a further clue about her real interests—opera. For the second time, the librarian urged her to look at the books in the music department and added that she might examine the collection of records and cassettes.

After an hour the patron returned to the reference librarian one more time, to say thank you. She then left with "new" books on Austrian history, literature, and travel, along with a few copies of *Opera News* and some examples of something really "positive" about the country—its music.

18. *What does SPC stand for? I need some case studies.*

An executive called her corporate library because she could not remember the meaning of SPC. She knew that it had something to do with statistics and that it is a management method.

The librarian checked a long "SPC" list in the *Acronyms, Initialisms and Abbreviations Dictionary* and found the correct entry: "Statistical Process Control."

"Yes, that's it! I need some case studies—you know, how it was implemented by specific companies."

Unfortunately, the librarian could not provide her with any quick answers because the computer used for online searching was not functioning and the arrival of the service people was not imminent. But the city's public library system had established a

Case Studies / 81

special business library in the financial district. It was pointed out that that library's collection is larger than the corporate library's so the text of articles would likely be retrieved from their large collection of business periodicals.

The business librarian was familiar with SPC and searched ABI/INFORM, MANAGEMENT CONTENTS, and TRADE AND INDUSTRY INDEX via DIALOG. Each database contained references to a number of relevant case studies.

> From MANAGEMENT CONTENTS: Jack B. ReVelle and Hugh Jordan Harrington, "Use of Statistical Process-Quality Control in the Defense Industries," *Industrial Engineering* (February 20, 1988): 36.
>
> Mehran Sepehri, "Manufacturing Realization at Harley-Davidson Motor Co.: Setup Times, Inventory Turns Reduced," *Industrial Engineering* (August 19, 1987): 86+.
>
> From ABI/INFORM: Klaus M. Blanche et al., "Process Control and People at General Motors' Delta Engine Plant," *Industrial Engineering*, 20 (March 1988): 24–30.
>
> Lisa Tocci, "SPC Continues to Win Converts in Packaging Field," *The Oil Daily* (April 20, 1988): B15.
>
> From TRADE AND INDUSTRY INDEX: Jim Hallinan, "SPC is More Than Making the Motions," *Paperboard Packaging* 73 (January 1988): 46+.
>
> Elizabeth Ben Daniel, "Using Statistical Process Control with Robotic Testing Improves Quality Level," *Industrial Engineering* 20 (February 1988): 26+.

Just as the search was being completed the executive returned to the desk (she was examining the collection while waiting for the results) and asked if the name "Edward Deming" could be searched. She remembered that he was important to the development of the SPC method.

"Deming" was searched in the same field (F) as "Statistical Process Control," using the same databases. A number of articles on W. Edwards Deming were located. Using only the last name proved efficient because the patron remembered the rest of the name incorrectly.

19. *I need an article from* Newsday *on freezing teeth.*

A patron, with frustration in her eyes, approached an urban public library's reference desk, gave her name, and said that she works for a dentist (as a hygienist). She explained that an article appeared in the "Discovery" section of *Newsday* (a New York City/Long Island newspaper) a few months before about freezing teeth for use in implantation at a later date. She, the doctor, and everyone else in the office remembered the article and thought that it had been clipped and saved. They had just about turned the office upside down but could not find it. The doctor had called the newspaper and found out that they do not provide telephone information service to the public. The newspaper's librarian referred her to the public library.

The hygienist wondered what the public library could do for her because she knew that no equivalent of the *New York Times Index* existed for *Newsday*.

The public librarian told the patron that *Newsday* is available on an online database vendor system called VU/TEXT and that it would be available in a month. But all was not lost! The patron was surprised to hear that the information was quite easy to get because the public library and the newspaper enjoy a cooperative relationship. After a five-minute telephone call, the information was given to the patron: Gene Messenger, "Tooth Transplants," in "Health Watch" (column), Discovery Section, (March 22, 1988): 10.

A very happy dental hygienist went to the periodicals room to retrieve the newspaper and photocopy the article.

20. *What did Tex Antoine say that got him fired from WABC-TV?*

This question was asked of one of the adult services librarians in a medium-sized public library serving an affluent community of approximately 250,000 people. The patron said that he remembered that sometime in the 1970s Antoine, an "Eyewitness News" weatherman, said something about rape and quoted Confucius. It was supposed to be a joke but the public was outraged by his bad taste.

The patron had looked at "a bunch of indexes" and a friend of his checked Bartlett's but neither of them found anything.

He was informed by the librarian that there are many quotation books available, some of them devoted to the words, remarks, and expressions of famous contemporary American personalities in politics, show business, sports, and so forth. The collection included quite a variety of quotation books because many patrons ask about who said what and when. A number of likely sources were selected and both the librarian and the patron began checking the indexes under "Antoine, Tex."

A reference was finally found in Rowes, *The Book of Quotes*, 217: "With rape so predominant in the news lately, it is well to remember the words of Confucius: 'If rape is inevitable, lie back and enjoy it.'"

The entry revealed key information about the event. Antoine had not been fired—he had been suspended, and the year was 1976.

The patron, a regular user, then requested a NEXIS search to quickly locate all the newspaper stories on the event. He remarked that he spends too much time satisfying his curiosity and did not want to take the time to search through the hard copy indexes.

The librarian logged on to NEXIS and selected the NEW YORK TIMES ABSTRACTS file (abstracts of stories from newspapers, magazines, and journals from January 1969) and did a name search. Eight references were retrieved, and all but one were about Antoine's remark. The most recent article announced his death on January 12, 1983.

21. *I'm looking for the institutional holdings of CMS Energy.*

A young business consultant and recent university graduate traveled to the business library of his (nearby) alma mater because he knew the collection intimately. He spent quite some time checking a variety of sources but could not find complete data or the most recent information. He went to the reference desk to ask for an online search of the DISCLOSURE database. The librarian told him that, as an alumnus, he would have to pay a special fee to be able to use the online service. Disappointment was soon replaced by hopefulness when he was referred to the city's public library—where he could have a search done for free.

As a matter of policy, ready reference searches were run immediately. The public librarian logged on to the DISCLOSURE/SPECTRUM OWNERSHIP database (via DIALOG), which was current to the month. The simple search by company name, "CO = CMS Energy?," resulted in one record. Format seven, institutional holdings, was selected and a list of seventy-six owners (plus the latest quarter change in shares, shares held, and filing date) was printed.

While the data were being printed, the patron asked if the librarian could do another quick search in the same database on the A&P food chain. He was sure that the company had been acquired by some foreign firm and needed the name.

Format eight, "Ownership by 5% Owners," revealed three: Haub, Erivan—West Germany; Tengelmann Warenhandelsgesellschaft—West Germany; Oppenheimer Group—United States.

The patron started to leave, but returned to the librarian. "I wonder if I could ask something that might sound silly." He was encouraged to state his new need. He said that he had heard that somebody from the "Leave It to Beaver" cast had recently died, but his friend disagreed with him. The librarian asked him to wait and logged on to NEXIS, selecting the NEW YORK TIMES FULL TEXT in the PAPERS file, entering: "Leave w/2 (within two words of) Beaver." One article, dated August 11, 1984, Section 1, 28 (certainly not recent) announced the death of Richard Deacon who played Lumpy Rutherford's father.

The patron's next thought was that it might have been Jerry Mathers. Using the same file, the librarian found no obituary, but an August 7, 1985 article (Section C, 19) stated that word of his death was just a rumor—Mathers is still alive and well!

22. *I am looking for information on the use of aspirin to prevent heart attacks.*

A student had run his own online search on BRS AFTER DARK, using a microcomputer located in his dormitory. He had successfully searched the NATIONAL NEWSPAPER INDEX and MAGAZINE INDEX. Using the terms "aspirin" and "heart adj (adjacent to) attacks," he located exactly what he wanted.

"Aspirin is Said to Help Heart Attack Survival," *New York Times,* March 31, 1988.

Leanne Kleinmann, "Half an Aspirin a Day May Keep a Heart Attack Away," *Health,* 20 (May 1988): 8.

He also needed the medical viewpoint and conducted the same search in MEDLINE. To his amazement, he retrieved only two citations, yet they did not seem to be what he needed. Rather than continue the search (his time allowance was just about expired anyway), he went to the library that night and asked the student assistant at the desk for some help.

The assistant suggested that he go to the online search service office the following morning to talk to the information specialist. The specialist examined his search results and called the student's attention to the term "myocardial infarction" mentioned in the two MEDLINE records.

"I should have thought of that, but I guess I didn't read too carefully." The student was assured that his searching technique would improve with experience.

Another database, PHARMACEUTICAL NEWS INDEX (available only via DIALOG), was mentioned as an excellent source for current information as it is updated weekly. The student wanted to do his own searching, but was told that he could not gain access to the PHARMACEUTICAL NEWS INDEX via BRS.

There was a week-long delay (because of other requests received before his) which was no problem for the student since he needed time to search MEDLINE and read all the articles he found in the general periodicals.

Meanwhile, the online search specialist logged on to DIALOG and searched the PHARMACEUTICAL NEWS INDEX using the statement: "aspirin and heart(w)attacks or myocardial infarction or mi." This strategy effectively retrieved all relevant records on the subject because one or the other of three terms were combined with the word "aspirin."

The student was notified of the completed search. When he arrived at the online search service office he enthusiastically announced his success with the MEDLINE search as well. He had gone to the university's medical library, as the search specialist had suggested, and photocopied a number of excellent reports. The student was convinced that the search in the PHARMACEUTICAL NEWS INDEX was well worth the fee. He was anxious to return to the medical library. He told the information specialist that he had really learned something—he now realized how important it is to think of different words and phrases when the one you are sure of fails. He added that his term paper "covered all angles" and should net him a good grade!

23. *What patents have been granted for muscle-testing devices in the years 1985 to 1988?*

This question was received in a law library located in a large city. The lawyer was asking on behalf of a business consultant who was both a friend and a client. His friend/client did try to find the information in his corporate library by checking through the *United States Patent and Trademark Office Official Gazette*. He admitted total defeat after he tried to battle his way through various lists of data, including different categories of patents granted, design patents granted, index of patentees, indices of reissue/reexamination/design, classification of patents, geographical index of residence of inventors, and so on. "The *Gazette* is published weekly, with annual indexes!"

The lawyer was used to obtaining material from online databases and guessed that a patent search would also be possible. However, the law library only provided access to LEXIS and WESTLAW, legal online search services. The librarian told the lawyer that the public library provides free access to DIALOG—and yes, there is a patent database available. This information was relayed to his client who changed his lunchtime plans immediately.

The pre-search interview revealed that the patron needed patent information for mechanical apparatus. When the CLAIMS/US PATENT ABSTRACTS database (via DIALOG) was selected, the patron decided to broaden his search to include the period covered by File 25—1982 to the present. The search statement was entered: "muscle (f) (in the same field as) test? (? = truncation to search for all words beginning with t-e-s-t)." The search was then limited to mechanical patents, using the delimiter "/m." Ten patents were filed from 1982 to the present and the full record was printed out for each, giving the name of the device, the inventor(s), patent application number and date, patent number and date, abstract, claim (purpose of the device), classification number, and so forth.

The patron thanked the librarian for easing the strain on his life, and selected those devices he was most interested in so that he could obtain copies of the patents from the Patent and Trademark Office in Washington, D.C.

24. *What are the issues concerning Japan and international trade for 1988?*

A college freshman began his research by looking through *Facts on File*, a source he was familiar with from high school. He found quite a number of references in the 1988 index by looking under "Japan—Monetary, Trade, Aid and Investment." He read the entries and jotted down the dates. Then the student located the newspapers and news magazines for those dates and photocopied a number of articles.

He retrieved more relevant material from INFOTRAC, as suggested by the periodicals librarian. But the student was not satisfied that he had found all relevant material and went to the computer service department to request an online search. The librarian/intermediary explained that too many articles would be retrieved from the NATIONAL NEWSPAPER INDEX, MAGAZINE INDEX, and NEWSEARCH because the topic is so "hot." To illustrate the problem, the search was run (without charge) to show the student how many articles would come up. The search statement "Japan? (? = truncation to include all variations of the word beginning with the letters J-a-p-a-n) (f) (within the same field as) trade and PY (publication year) = 1988" yielded 582 articles in the NATIONAL NEWSPAPER INDEX, seventy-one in MAGAZINE INDEX, and 326 in NEWSEARCH.

The information specialist suggested the student then go to the public library because they offer a free online search service and might print out at least some of the most recent material.

To his surprise, the student discovered that the public library could do a search for all of 1988, using NEXIS BUSABS (Business Abstracts); this database focuses on business data only. The search statement used was "Trade and Japan! ("!" is used by NEXIS to indicate truncation) and date is 1988." The results provided the student with an excellent bibliography. He also learned that he could save money on online searches by using the public library's free service.

25. *I am looking for some information on NOTA BENE.*

A German professor decided to forsake his treasured typewriter and take the plunge into the world of technology so that he would be able to speed up his writing efforts in order to meet deadlines and become more productive. He also heard that the editing process is less painful with a word processing system. He had purchased an IBM-compatible microcomputer recently, but could not decide on a word processing program. He asked his "automated" colleagues for their recommendations. Two of them were enthusiastic about WORDSTAR because they had been using it for years. But three others told him that "he will experience the ultimate in writing ease with NOTA BENE."

The German department's secretary agreed with the majority and handed him an informational brochure that listed all the wonderful features of the program, along with the price and the name and address of the publisher: Dragonfly Software, 285 W. Broadway, Suite 500, New York, NY 10013. She added that the Modern Language Association recommends it highly.

The professor felt that an outline of the special features of the program was not enough information for an intelligent decision. He therefore decided that he needed a more detailed description of the program. The department secretary recommended that he go to the university computer center.

The student assistant at the desk maintained a collection of computer magazines and had created an index to hardware and software review articles. A review of version 3.0 appeared in *PC Magazine,* February 29, 1988, 30; one of version 2.0 was in *PC Magazine,* July 21, 1987, 43. The August 10, 1987 issue of *InfoWorld* included a review (p. 53+) headlined, "Nota Bene; Word Processor Caters to Academic Community; Footnoting, Indexing, Style Manual References Among Features."

The two issues of *PC Magazine* were available in the computer center but *InfoWorld* was missing. Since the professor thought that the article (based on the title) might be important to him, he was anxious to obtain a copy of it and asked where he might go to get it. The student assistant referred him to the science library, but the effort was futile since the same issue was missing from that collection as well.

The science librarian had two suggestions. The first, an interlibrary loan, was not very attractive because the professor wanted to obtain a copy quickly. The second, a trip to the university's business library to obtain a print-out of the full text of *InfoWorld* from the NEXIS papers file, was a better alternative. However, the business librarian apologized for not being able to do the search for him because the printer had just broken.

There was yet another alternative! NEXIS is available at the city's public library. A telephone call (made by the librarian) verified that their equipment was functioning and that they do take telephone requests. The telephone receiver was handed over to the professor, who stated his request once again and was interviewed by the public library's online search specialist.

The professor's search was run while he was in transit to the public library. He approached the reference desk, stated his name, and was handed a print-out of the full text of the *InfoWorld* review. The professor concluded that the time he took to obtain the article was worthwhile. The article was quite informative and convinced him that this wordprocessing system would do the most for him. On his way back to his office he stopped at the computer store near the campus and purchased NOTA BENE—at a discounted price for university faculty.

List of Sources Cited

ABI/INFORM (database). Louisville, Ky.: UMI/Data Courier, August 1971–present.
Acronyms, Initialisms and Abbreviations Dictionary. Julie E. Towell and Helen E. Sheppard, eds. Detroit: Gale Research, 1987.
An Exaltation of Larks or The Venereal Game. James Lipton. New York: Grossman, 1968.
ASSOCIATED PRESS POLITICAL (APOLIT) SERVICE. (NEXIS database). Dayton, Ohio: Mead Data Central, current.
Blakiston's Gould Medical Dictionary. 4th ed. New York: McGraw-Hill, 1979.

Book of Quotes. Barbara Rowes. New York: E. P. Dutton, 1979.
Buchsbaum's Complete Handbook of Practical Electronic Reference Data. 2nd ed. Englewood Cliffs, N.J.: Prentice Hall, 1981.
BUSINESS ABSTRACTS (BUSABS) LIBRARY (NEXIS database). Dayton, Ohio: Mead Data Central, current.
CLAIMS/U.S. PATENT ABSTRACTS (database). Alexandria, Va.: IFL/Plenum Data Company, 1950–present.
Columbia University College of Physicians and Surgeons Complete Home Medical Guide. Donald F. Tapley et al., eds. New York: Crown, 1985.
COMPREHENSIVE CORE MEDICAL LIBRARY (database). Latham, N.Y.: BRS Information Technologies, 1982–present.
Dictionary of Mythology, Folklore and Symbols. New York: Scarecrow, 1962.
DISCLOSURE/SPECTRUM OWNERSHIP (database). Bethesda, Md.: Disclosure Information Group, current.
Electronic Encyclopedia (CD-ROM). Danbury, Conn.: Grolier, 1986.
Encyclopedia Americana. Danbury, Conn.: Grolier, 1988.
Encyclopedia of American Religions. 2nd ed. J. Gordon Melton. Detroit: Gale Research, 1987.
Facts on File: Weekly World News Digest with Cumulative Index. New York: Facts on File, 1988.
GEOREF (database). Alexandria, Va.: American Geological Institute, 1785–present.
"Highlights of the Online Database Field: New Technologies for Online." Martha Williams. In *National Online Meeting Proceedings—1988.* Medford, N.J.: Learned Information, 1988.
Library of Congress. Charles A. Goodrum. New York: Praeger, 1974.
Library of Congress: A Picture Story of the World's Largest Library. Gene Gurney. New York: Crown, 1966.
LISA (Library and Information Science Abstracts) (database). London: Library Association Publishing, 1969–present.
MAGAZINE INDEX (database). Foster City, Calif.: Information Access Company, 1959–present.

92 / Personnel Needs and Changing Reference Services

MANAGEMENT CONTENTS (database). Foster City, Calif.: Information Access Company, September 1974–present.

MEDLINE (database). Bethesda, Md.: U.S. National Library of Medicine, 1966–present.

MICROCOMPUTER SOFTWARE & HARDWARE GUIDE (database). New York: R. R. Bowker, current.

NATIONAL NEWSPAPER INDEX (database). Foster City, Calif.: Information Access Company, 1979–present.

NEW YORK TIMES (NEXIS service full-text database). Dayton, Ohio: Mead Data Central, June 1980–present.

NEWSEARCH (database). Foster City, Calif.: Information Access Company, current month.

Official Gazette of the United States Patent and Trademark Office. Washington, D.C.: Government Printing Office, weekly.

PHARMACEUTICAL NEWS INDEX (database). Louisville, Ky.: UMI/Data Courier, 1974–present.

PSYCINFO (database). Washington, D.C.: American Psychological Association, 1967–present.

RELIGION INDEX (database). Chicago: American Theological Library Association, 1975–present.

Standard Dictionary of Computers and Information Processing. Martin H. Weik. New York: Hayden, 1969.

Stedman's Medical Dictionary. 24th ed. Baltimore: Williams & Wilkins, 1982.

Symbolism: A Comprehensive Dictionary. Steven Olderr. Jefferson, N.C.: McFarland, 1986.

Taber's Cyclopedic Medical Dictionary. 15th ed. Clayton L. Thomas, ed. Philadelphia: F. A. Davis, 1985.

TRADE & INDUSTRY INDEX (database). Foster City, Calif.: Information Access Company, 1981–present.

Trade Names Dictionary. 6th ed. Detroit: Gale Research, 1988.

Trade Names Dictionary: Supplement to the 6th Edition. Detroit: Gale Research, 1988.

TRADEMARKSCAN-FEDERAL (database). North Quincy, Mass.: Thomson & Thomson, 1884–present.

TRADEMARKSCAN-STATE (database). North Quincy, Mass: Thomson & Thomson, November 1986–present.

World Book Encyclopedia. Chicago: World Book, 1988.

4
Evaluating Reference

Libraries should be able to offer enhanced reference service by providing more personnel and having the opportunity to train staff and patrons in reference skills and in mastering computerized access routes. For this to be made possible, administrations have to be convinced of the importance of quality reference service to the health and vitality of the library as a whole. Too many librarians do not make dramatic and compelling statements based on hard evidence to justify a budget for computerized resources, staff enlargement, continuing education programs for personnel, and teaching and counseling sessions for end-users. The common, and unfortunate, action, particularly in public libraries, is to count the number of questions received as a way of showing how heavily reference service is used. But this figure is not evidence of the quality or value of the service provided because it says nothing about patron satisfaction, the knowledge and skill needed to answer each query fully and correctly, the accuracy of the answers, and the resources used or needed to retrieve information. The argument for an adequate budget to support expanding resources that include electronic tools, additional professionals, and ongoing staff and end-user training programs must also include clear proof of the value of the reference function to individual library users, along with the impact of this service on the future of the library as a major source of information. For example, analysis of the use of automated information retrieval systems should reveal that with it, the use of traditional sources tends to increase; a study of end-user searching patterns should show that as it increases so does the demand for mediated online searching—making the need for qualified professionals and expansion of reference service greater.

Clearly, automated information retrieval systems and end-user searching have had a profound effect on reference work in all types of libraries. Continuous evaluation of reference service, staff performance, personnel and patron educational and training programs, and use of resources is imperative in order to determine how the addition or absence of access to electronic resources influences the ability to fulfill library goals and functions. The process of ongoing assessment is difficult because it involves a great deal of time for planning, study, and analysis. No standard evaluatory method has been developed that fits every situation in every library—there are just too many variables to consider.

- Patrons: research faculty, technologists, average citizens, professionals, graduates, undergraduates, high school or elementary school students.
- Library size: university, college, special library, central or branch of a public library system, small remote library in a cooperative or federated system.
- Demographics of the population served; income, educational level, occupation.
- Staff: size, professional education, degree of dedication, motivation, knowledge of traditional and electronic resources, ability to manage collections, and lobby for budgets and programs.
- Reference service policy: time spent per patron, completeness of answers, interviewing, counseling practice, directional help or full assistance, mediated searching for a fee or free, end-user searching and total support.
- Attention to users: librarians too busy to effectively satisfy all users.
- Size and scope of the collection.
- Qualifications of nonprofessionals: ability to provide useful and correct assistance to patrons, and search effectively using manual or computerized end-user systems.

96 / Personnel Needs and Changing Reference Service

- Formal in-service training in relation to the success rate.
- Job satisfaction and patron satisfaction.
- Manual or online searching and the relationship to the number of people served, and to the increase or decrease of the workload.
- Number of full-time staff members: effect of staff size on the number of manual or automated searches completed.
- Ability to access online databases in relation to the adequacy of the book and periodical collections.
- Availability of electronic resources and the size of the staff.
- Searching time and the presence of a human versus an automated intermediary (end-user system).
- User perception of service: whether or not information is usually found when the librarian helps.
- Level of communication between users and staff.
- User judgment of professionals' qualifications: expertise, completeness of answers, attitude toward patrons.
- Availability of library instructional programs: tours, lectures, orientation talks, individual tutoring, counseling, guidance, and their effect on library use.
- Extent of professional commitment to expanding knowledge of resources or outside sources: level of interest in study and consideration of options/approaches to individual requests, and improving interview skills to discover patron real need.
- Degree of emphasis placed on accuracy and the development of the "we-are-here-to-help-you" atmosphere.

Since the process of continuous assessment is complicated and multifaceted, it requires evaluators who are experienced reference librarians, professional searchers/information specialists, skilled developers of assessment methods, and talented decision makers—with the ability to make intelligent, objective choices and recommendations that are based on library goals and focused on the real needs of its clientele.

Understandably, many librarians and administrators are reluctant to commit themselves to a program of in-depth and constant evaluation because they fear it is too time-consuming, expensive, and idealistic—taking away much of the time needed to do "real" reference work. In truth, it is impossible to develop or maintain consistently high quality reference service without looking at what is going on and examining ways to improve and enhance resources and staff responses to patron needs.

Effective management includes organization and reorganization of reference service, resource development, staff selection, education, and training, the teaching, training, and counseling of dependent patrons as well as end-users, budget management and justification, and measurement of user satisfaction. As new patron needs are identified and anticipated, they must be met by providing access to new print and electronic resources. Increased user demand must be accommodated by hiring new, qualified personnel. At the same time, existing staff must be given the opportunity to develop new skills and reference expertise.

Successful management is therefore absolutely tied to in-depth analysis and evaluation of service. Exactly what is involved? The following is a basic outline to assess service.

The Staff

Analysis of the reference product provided by the staff can be achieved by utilizing different methods of measuring, recording, and reporting on the quality of service that are practical and as accurate and reliable as possible.

Direct Observation

Direct observation by supervisors of personnel in action should reveal areas of performance excellence and deficiencies; a variety of questions should be answered:

98 / Personnel Needs and Changing Reference Service

- How well are they succeeding in connecting users to information?
- How effectively are they teaching patrons about the library's resources?
- How easily is rapport achieved with users?
- What level of assistance is given to individual users?
- Is the staff giving more than directions and short answers? Is there more pointing to resources than talking with patrons to explain them?
- Are they actively engaging in expanding their knowledge of traditional and electronic resources and services (both within and outside of the library system)?
- Are alternatives being readily explored when responding to particular queries?
- Are reference interview skills sufficiently developed to get at patrons' real needs?
- Are accurate and complete answers being given?
- Is an effort being made to find better or more complete or current data and make accurate referrals, when appropriate?

Staff Surveys and Meetings

Staff surveys, informal meetings, and conferences are important means of getting feedback. The subjects will range widely: the success of in-house educational and training programs, collection weaknesses, patron needs/demands/complaints, the benefits and deficiencies of established and new computerized systems and services, equipment problems, newly discovered sources of information, policy and procedural problems and suggested revisions, trends in use, the performance of support staff nonprofessionals, and so forth.

Nonprofessionals (e.g., volunteers, student assistants, library interns) who are assigned reference duties must be observed continuously. If carefully selected and vigorously taught and trained, they should be able to:

Evaluating Reference / 99

- answer routine questions of a directional or informational nature, e.g., library hours, programs, book sale schedule, branch locations, location of special collections, online search service(s), database vendor systems available, location of agencies, special libraries, public/academic libraries, associations, restrooms, and more
- recognize types of questions asked at the reference desk and refer research queries, problem questions, or any other type of inquiry to professional staff, rather than attempt to answer questions for which they have no expertise
- provide assistance in the use of the collection and the sources—useful in off hours when no professional staff is available and the reference desk is staffed by a student assistant with subject expertise
- answer catalog use questions and assist patrons in locating specific titles, authors, or subjects
- assist patrons in locating and retrieving sources from reserve shelves or open stack areas
- set up a computer system for patrons by turning it on, inserting the software or compact disc, and calling up the first menu screen
- help the patron with the operation of a computer system by explaining the steps to follow, the on-screen and written instructions, the various function keys, the layout of the keyboard, entering search terms and combining them, Boolean logic, how to start a new search, or sign off
- troubleshoot equipment problems: for example, what to do if the program freezes, the patron is disconnected from an online system, the printer fails to print, and so forth

Support staff must be acutely aware of their own limitations and of policies, procedures, the location of reference sources, and existence of referral libraries, offices, outside agencies, and professional contacts. They must be provided with the necessary aids—maps and informational material about the library or system, lists of contacts within and outside of the library or system, library directories, directories of available automated systems, accessible databases, vendor help lines, associations, cultural institutions, and so on. They must learn to pay close attention to individual user requests and, if necessary, respond by providing a referral to a professional available at a later time or at a different location.

Again, continuous assessment of nonprofessionals is necessary to ensure that the best reference service possible is available at all times. Sometimes it is difficult to staff reference desks with professionals (e.g., the graveyard shift in a university library); the next best choice is alert, interested, and well-trained nonprofessionals.

Statistics

By comparing various combinations of statistical data that are collected by unobtrusive observation, regular patron or staff surveys, or by using different statistics forms developed to record the frequency of occurrence of specific reference activities, certain assumptions can be proved or disproved, thereby identifying trends in reference service. A variety of data, descriptive of different aspects of service, should be gathered by staff as a part of the normal routine. Regular analysis of the statistical significance of these data determines how reference service should be expanded or made more efficient. The information to be collected should include:

- Patterns of use: who uses the library; when is it used—daily, weekly, monthly, irregularly, as the first or last resort; whether used independently or the librarian is asked for help; busy periods are avoided because it is difficult to obtain help, and so forth.
- User demographics: age level, occupation, school years completed, family income, per capita income, and other factors that could influence patron information needs and the available resources and reference service.

- Level of use: general information, ready-reference, research.
- Users' major fields of interest or research.
- Patron library experience: level of satisfaction with the collection, referrals, and staff assistance on a scale of one (least) to five (most).
- Computer knowledge and experience: none, minimal, moderate, extensive; what systems are or have been used and for what purpose—data management, word processing, online searching, and so forth.
- Amount of time spent on research and per research session: the time the end-user spends from logon to logoff; the time the staff spends assisting patrons or as an intermediary searcher.
- Patron-perceived value of training, orientation, counseling sessions or demonstrations: degree of usefulness on a scale of one (least) to five (most).
- Databases and systems searched and those most frequently searched: record statistics on search strategy sheets and/or brief patron survey forms; analyze detailed vendor invoices.
- End-user experience with particular system(s): ease of use, need for assistance, value of data retrieved, and overall judgment of the system(s) on a scale of one (least) to five (most).
- Types of queries asked.
- Periods of heaviest library use: number of questions received each hour or half hour, type of questions (ready-reference, informational, directional, community information, research), subject areas, number of professionals available, length of queues.
- Degree of user satisfaction with service: very dissatisfied, dissatisfied, neutral, satisfied, very satisfied.

These statistical figures provide answers to certain questions, including the following:

- Is the collection (traditional and electronic) adequate to fulfill the majority of patron requests?

- Are patrons getting the staff assistance they need?
- To what degree are they able to use the collection independently?
- Do patrons know what the resources of the library are?
- Do patrons realize that the librarians can access resources outside the library?
- Do staff expertise, knowledge, and experience have any relationship to the amount of time spent on a research session?
- Does staff searching in more than one database increase or decrease their precision and/or rate of success?
- Is the degree of patron satisfaction lower during busy periods?
- Do patrons tend to ask questions about subjects outside of the scope of the library's collection? If so, are other print sources or databases accessible or are referrals readily made?
- Do subject specialists tend to search databases outside of their field of expertise to answer a particular query?
- Are they aware of the limitations of CD-ROM products and online databases?
- If users want to do their own searching, are they encouraged to do so by the staff? Are they better at it after formal instruction or one-on-one sessions?
- Do they like CD-ROM databases or gateways/front-ends? Are they willing to pay for online access or do they settle for free CD-ROM searching?
- Do patrons tend to be more successful in locating needed information if the librarian helps?
- Do users with experience with particular systems want to search other systems more readily? If so, does the rate of precision increase?
- Are staff and users continuously reminded of alternative sources of information as well as other services, such as regional/central libraries, cooperative systems, networks, interlibrary loan, or telefacsimile services?

Peer Review

Peer review should be used in a constructive way to evaluate different approaches to answering reference queries, methods of handling problem searches, the benefits of various computerized tools and print sources, the value and usefulness of system enhancements, additional databases, and so on.

Staff might hold weekly, bi-weekly or monthly meetings to discuss observations made of each other's approaches to individual patrons—whether the users were given enough attention, why particular routes to answers were chosen, and what might have been a better or more direct approach. If conducted in an informal and supportive atmosphere, these review sessions can be quite valuable. In my experience, those involved have willingly shared information and suggestions and engaged in constructive criticism. I have never had to assume the role of a general in a battlefield.

Self-Evaluation

Like peer review, self-evaluation is a way of stepping back to take a critical look at performance quality:

- Do I have a thorough knowledge and understanding of print sources, databases, and automated systems?
- Do I keep abreast of technological developments by taking time to read the literature?
- Do I establish a rapport with patrons quickly and easily and invite questions, or do some or all patrons annoy me?
- Do I listen closely to patron requests, problems, and needs and work at finding out what the real need is?
- Do I pay more attention to users with research projects that interest me and give others short shrift?
- Have I chosen the most efficient route to the needed data—print sources, online, referrals, or a combination of resources?

- Is the information retrieved (by me or the end-user) accurate, current, and sufficiently detailed?
- Have I invited feedback and willingly accepted new information or an additional question?
- Have I negotiated with a patron concerning a complicated search, rerun a search, clearly explained the findings, and invited a return visit?
- What other questions might I have asked to increase user satisfaction?

The Users

Important decisions about reference service are based on patron surveys of staff performance and library resources. End-user assessment of the adequacy of the collection, the value of automated products, and available staff support should be recorded. Short questionnaires that can be completed by the user are effective. The responses provide significant data on user success rates in relation to the amount and type of assistance given by the staff, usefulness of computerized tools, ease of use of automated end-user systems, satisfaction with the data retrieved, relevance of the information found, the value of library training and orientation programs, the success of professional counseling and support, the clarity of staff instructions and system documentation, overall user satisfaction, and more.

The Resources

Print Sources

Judgment of the hard copy collection should be based on an analysis of present and predicted future need. The effectiveness of the print collection must be continuously assessed by examining titles for currency, accuracy, format, ease of use, subjects covered, depth of coverage, uniqueness, etc.

If a title is not used, it should be discarded; if it is seldom used, it should be transferred to an appropriate library where there is a need. A title with an old publication date should be checked in *Books in Print* for a newer edition or a similar title that is more up-to-date. Sometimes a book will be the only one of its kind available. If the content is not outdated (i.e., books of origins, mythology, symbols), it should certainly be retained, with the hope that it might be eventually expanded and reprinted. Also, if one of a number of books covering the same subject has material not included in the others, it should be retained.

Statistics should be kept on the use and usefulness of print sources, for example, whether or not answers to queries were easily found, if the data were sufficiently complete, when online databases were needed to supplement the information, and when the hard copy sources failed. At the same time, choices of automated systems, databases, CD-ROM products, new hardware and software, and system enhancements must be carefully judged in order to make correct decisions and recommendations concerning acquisition or rejection.

Online Databases

The value of individual online databases should be determined by considering a variety of factors and offerings:

- subject coverage in relation to user needs/benefits, i.e., the ability to retrieve information that cannot otherwise be found easily, if at all, and the ability to combine concepts to retrieve data quickly and effectively
- completeness of subject coverage
- currency, that is frequency of updates: monthly, weekly, daily, or every fifteen minutes (the case with some wire services)
- retrospective coverage: current year only, last five, ten or more years
- format: full text, citations only, citations and abstracts

- search features: Boolean operators, controlled vocabulary, key word, nested logic, global searching, the ability to search multiple files at the same time (e.g., DIALOG ONESEARCH or NEXIS OMNI), and others
- cost of searching and retrieval, print charges, database surcharges
- predicted usage: online is recommended when subject is not in great demand because no costs are involved if the database(s) is not used
- availability of other sources that are just as good, e.g., printed indexes, CD-ROM databases

Database Systems and Services

New or added database systems and services should be assessed by consideration of a variety of factors, including the following:

- equipment needed (microcomputer, laser printer, modem, etc.) and whether or not the equipment is dedicated to one system or database only
- subscription costs
- structure of the system—command language, interactive, menu-driven or front-end
- vendor training and support availability
- type of documentation available—thesauri, quick search aids, templates
- database coverage—in-depth subject coverage, general periodicals, specialized journals
- uniqueness of databases, as compared to those already subscribed to
- frequency of updates, system upgrades, and enhancements
- predicted usefulness to patrons, based on analysis of queries received by users

CD-ROM Products

CD-ROM products are attractive alternative search tools because they have the advantage of a predictable cost, and the unlimited searching of indexes, directories, encyclopedias, and other fulltext sources without the anxiety attached to online systems and connect-time fees. They save searching time in some cases because they offer increased access to subjects by allowing searching with more access points than are possible in printed indexes. The use of Boolean operators makes it possible to conduct more complex searches than are possible using printed indexes. CD-ROM databases also save searching time because the need for multiple look-ups in print sources is eliminated. Can end-users really search without any formal instruction? Ease of use varies and generally, all users require some instruction and training.

There are many factors to consider when assessing CD-ROM products. Among them are the following:

- subscription costs and cost effectiveness: for heavily used databases such as READER'S GUIDE TO PERIODICAL LITERATURE, ERIC, ABI/INFORM, NATIONAL NEWSPAPER INDEX, etc. (The CD-ROM choice is not practical for little-used subjects, and where print or online is a more effective choice.)
- equipment needs and compatibility with current equipment: If a particular compact disc does not run on the hardware the library already has, a dedicated work station or an additional microcomputer system to support another CD-ROM drive is necessary. The required funds and space to house the additional equipment may not be readily available. Systems that support multiple compact discs are more cost-effective and practical.
- frequency of equipment maintenance
- speed of data retrieval
- currency: as current or more current than print counterpart, e.g., BOOKS IN PRINT PLUS is updated quarterly, whereas the print counterpart is an annual

- accuracy and ease of use: indexing quality, menu screen clarity, help screens, search options, response time, and so forth
- telecommunications links available (If a library is located in a remote area, making a long distance call necessary when dialing to get online, then CD-ROM is an economical choice.)
- value to staff and end-users as an inexpensive learning tool to gain expertise in database searching

The evaluation process requires professionals to keep a clearly focused eye on new developments and their predicted benefits/ potential for enhancing reference. For example, new enhanced communications software products with more efficiency and better options built in; fast document delivery with telefacsimile as an alternative to interlibrary loan; hardware and software improvements, such as multi-user CD-ROM systems; the addition of graphics to databases; the use of hypertext to interface across different disciplines; artificial intelligence possibilities; the linking of libraries via local area networks.

Clearly, the ability to provide quality reference service depends on continuous evaluation of every aspect of the process, from the selection of sources to the education of staff to the satisfaction of the users. It is a complex job that requires time to keep up with the increasing rate of change of available technologies and to develop methods of gathering data, analyze findings, and justify decisions and recommendations.

Unfortunately, the need for ongoing assessment causes problems for some libraries because budgets are limited, the need for special knowledge and expertise required to do the job successfully is not fully appreciated, and the significance of in-depth evaluation of library service is not yet fully realized. Problems exist in convincing administrators that the effort is invaluable because it yields solid data (rather than fuzzy assumptions) on the quality of reference service. A well-planned, extensive, and ongoing evaluatory process, complete with sufficient qualified staff to ensure its continuance, is not terribly impractical. Rather, it is the best defense against obsolescence and poor performance.

Bibliography

Anderson, Charles. "The Limits of Reference." *RQ* 27 (Winter 1986), 147–50.

Auster, Ethel, ed. *Managing Online Reference Services*. New York: Neal-Schuman, 1986.

Auster, Ethel and Lawton, Stephen B. "Search Interview Techniques and Information Gain as Antecedents of User Satisfaction with Online Bibliographic Retrieval." *Journal of the American Society for Information Science* 35 (March 1984), 90–103.

Ballard, Thomas. "The Information Age and the Public Library." *Wilson Library Bulletin* 62 (June 1988), 74–78.

Bates, Marcia J. "How to Use Information Search Tactics Online." *Online* 11 (May 1987), 47–54.

Bearman, Toni Carbo, ed. "Educating the Future Information Professional." *Library Hi Tech* 18 (Summer 1987), 27–40.

Benham, Frances and Powel, Ronald R. *Success in Answering Reference Questions: Two Studies*. Metuchen, N.J.: Scarecrow, 1987.

Bowen, Charles. *Smarter Telecommunications*. New York: Bantam, 1985.

Brownmiller, Sara et al. "Online-Ready-Reference Searching in an Academic Library." *RQ* 24 (Spring 1985), 320–26.

Co, Francisca. "CD-ROM and the Library: Problems and Prospects." *Small Computers in Libraries* 7 (November 1987), 42–49.

Conger, Lucinda D. "Why Online is Not Obsolete." *Database* 11 (August 1988), 110–13.

Connolly, Bruce. "Looking Backward—CD-ROM and the Academic Library of the Future." *Online* 11 (May 1987), 56–61.

Corbin, John. *Developing Computer-Based Library Systems*. Phoenix, Ariz.: Oryx Press, 1981.

Cornick, Donna. "Being an End-User Is Not For Everyone." *Online* 13 (March 1989), 49–54.

110 / Bibliography

Cummins, Thompson R. "Demand Analysis: Inputs, Outputs, Outcomes, and Productivity." *Public Libraries* 27 (Spring 1988), 10–13.

Dalrymple, Prudence W. "Closing the Gap: The Role of the Librarian in Online Searching." *RQ* 24 (Winter 1984), 177–85.

Directory of Online Databases. 9 (July 1988). New York: Cuadra/Elsevier, 1988.

Dow, Victoria E. and Kriebel, Gail. "WILSONDISC: Training the Trainer." *National Online Meeting Proceedings—1988.* Medford, N.J.: Learned Information, 1988.

Dowlin, Kenneth. *The Electronic Library: The Promise and the Process.* New York: Neal-Schuman, 1984.

Drake, Miriam A. "Library 2000—Georgia Tech: A Glimpse of Information Delivery Now and in the Year 2000." *Online* 11 (November 1987), 45–48.

Encyclopedia of Information Systems and Services. 3 vols. Detroit: Gale Research, 1988.

Fayen, Emily Gallup. "The Answer Machine and Direct Connect: Do-It-Yourself Searching in Libraries." *Online* 12 (September 1988), 13–21.

Fenichel, Carol H. and Hogan, Thomas. *Online Searching: A Primer.* Marlton, N.J.: Learned Information, 1981.

Frank, Donald G. "Management of Student Assistants in a Public Services Setting of an Academic Library." *RQ* 24 (Fall 1984), 51–57.

Gelfand, Julia. "Professional Development for Reference and Adult Services Librarians." *RQ* 24 (Summer 1985), 402–3.

Gers, Ralph and Seward, Lillie J. "Improving Reference Performance: Results of a Statewide Study." *Library Journal* 110 (November 1, 1985), 32–5.

Glossbrenner, Alfred. *Complete Handbook of Personal Computer Communications.* New York: St. Martin's Press, 1985.

———. *How to Look it Up Online.* New York: St. Martin's Press, 1987.

Greiner, Joy M. "The Role of Nonprofessionals in Small Public Libraries." *Public Libraries* 27 (Summer 1988), 76–78.

Hansen, Carol. *Microcomputer User's Guide to Information Online.* Hasbrouck Heights, N.J.: Hayden, 1984.

Harter, Stephen P. and Fenichel, Carol H. "Online Searching in Library Education." *Journal of Education for Librarianship* 23 (Summer 1982), 3–22.

Harter, Stephen P. and Jackson, Susan M. "Optical Disc Systems in Libraries: Problems and Issues." *RQ* 27 (Summer 1988), 516–27.

Hawkins, Donald T. "Applications of Artificial Intelligence (AI) and Expert Systems for Online Searching." *Online* 12 (January 1988), 31–43.

Hawley, George S. *The Referral Process in Libraries: A Characterization and an Exploration of Related Factors.* Metuchen, N.J.: The Scarecrow Press, 1987.

Heim, Kathleen M. "Adult Services as Reflective of the Changing Role of the Public Library. *RQ* 27 (Winter 1986), 180–99.

Hernon, Peter. "Utility Measures, Not Performance Measures, for Library Reference Service." *RQ* 26 (Summer 1987), 449–59.

Hilchey, Susan E. and Hurych, Jitka M. "User Satisfaction or User Acceptance? Statistical Evaluation of an Online Reference Service." *RQ* 24 (Summer 1985), 452–59.

Hitchingham, Eileen and Titus, Elizabeth. "A Survey of Database Use at the Reference Desk." *Online* 8 (March 1984), 44–50.

Hoffmann, Ellen. "Managing Automation: A Process, Not a Project." *Library Hi Tech* 6 (1988), 45–54.

Hoover, Ryan E. ed. *Online Search Strategies.* White Plains, N.Y.: Knowledge Industries, 1982.

Hu, Chengren. "An Evaluation of a Gateway System for Automated Online Database Selection." *National Online Meeting Proceedings—1988.* Medford, N.J.: Learned Information, 1988.

Humphrey, Susanne M. and Melloni, Biagio John. *Databases: A Primer for Retrieving Information by Computer.* Englewood Cliffs, N.J.: Prentice-Hall, 1986.

Jahoda, Gerald and Braunagel, Judith Schiek. *The Librarian and Reference Queries: A Systematic Approach.* New York: Academic Press, 1980.

Jahoda, Gerald and Olson, Paul E. "Analyzing the Reference Process." *RQ* 12 (Winter 1972), 148–56.

Janke, Richard V. "Online After Six: End User Searching Comes of Age." *Online* 8 (November 1984), 15–29.

———. "Presearch Counseling for Client Searchers (End-Users)." *Online* 9 (September 1985), 13–26.

Katz, Bill, ed. and comp. *Reference and Information Services: A Reader for Today.* Metuchen, N.J.: Scarecrow Press, 1986.

Katz, Bill and Fraley, Ruth A., eds. *Evaluation of Reference Services.* New York: Haworth, 1984.

112 / Bibliography

———. *Library Instruction and Reference Services*. New York: Haworth, 1984.

———. *Reference Services Today: From Interview to Burnout*. New York: Haworth, 1986.

Katz, William A. *Introduction to Reference Work*. 2 vols. 4th ed. New York: McGraw-Hill, 1982.

Kesselman, Martin and Watstein, Sarah B., eds. *End-User Searching: Services and Providers*. Chicago: American Library Association, 1988.

King, Geraldine B. "The Reference Interview." *RQ* 12 (Winter 1972), 157–60.

Kohl, David F. *Reference Services and Library Instruction: A Handbook for Library Management*. Santa Barbara, Calif.: ABC-CLIO, 1985.

Lee, Joann H. *Online Searching: The Basics, Settings and Management*. Littleton, Colo.: Libraries Unlimited, 1984.

Littlejohn, Alice C. "End-user Searching in an Academic Library—The Students' View." *RQ* 26 (Summer 1987), 460–66.

Lowe, John B. "Gambling on CD-ROM." *Library Journal* 113 (July 1988), 37–39.

Markham, Marilyn J., Stirling, Keith H., and Smith, Nathan M. "Librarian Self-Disclosure and Patron Satisfaction in the Reference Interview." *RQ* 22 (Summer 1983), 369–74.

Michell, Gillian and Harris, Roma M. "Evaluating the Reference Interview: Some Factors Influencing Patrons and Professionals." *RQ* 27 (Fall 1987), 95–105.

Miko, Chris J. "Ensuring End-User Quality Control: An Academic Model." *National Online Meeting Proceedings—1988*. Medford, N.J.: Learned Information, 1988.

Murr, Lawrence E. and Williams, James B. "The Roles of the Future Library." *Library Hi Tech* 19 (Fall 1987), 7–23.

Newlin, Barbara. *Answers Online: Your Guide to Informational Data Bases*. Berkeley, Calif.: Osborne McGraw-Hill, 1985.

O'Hanlon, Nancyanne. "Up the Down Staircase: Establishing Library Instruction Programs for Teachers." *RQ* 27 (Summer 1988), 528–33.

Palmer, Roger C. *Online Reference and Information Retrieval*. Littleton, Colo.: Libraries Unlimited, 1987.

Quint, Barbara. "Connect Time." *Wilson Library Bulletin* 62 (November 1987), 57–59.

Reynolds, Dennis. *Library Automation: Issues and Applications*. New York: Bowker, 1985.

Riechel, Rosemarie. *Improving Telephone Information and Reference Service in Public Libraries*. Hamden, Conn.: Library Professional Publication, The Shoe String Press, 1987.

Rothstein, Samuel. "The Making of a Reference Librarian." *Library Trends* 31 (Winter 1983), 375–99.

———. "The Measurement and Evaluation of Reference Service." *Library Trends* 12 (January 1964), 456–72.

———. "Professional Staff in Canadian University Libraries." *Library Journal* 111 (November 1, 1986), 31–34.

Shaw, Debora. "Information Literacy and Education of Information Professionals." *Bulletin of the American Society for Information Science* 14 (December/January 1988), 35.

Sievert, Mary Ellen et al. "Investigating Computer Anxiety in an Academic Library." *Information Technology and Libraries* 7 (September 1988), 243–52.

Sigel, Efrem et al. *Books, Libraries and Electronics: Essays on the Future of Written Communication*. White Plains, N.Y.: Knowledge Industry, 1982.

Smith, Karen E. "Hypertext—Linking to the Future." *Online* 12 (March 1988), 32–40.

Snow, Maxine Leeds. "Removing the Mystery: Training the End User to Search." *National Online Meeting Proceedings—1988*. Medford, N.J.: Learned Information, 1988.

Stabler, Karen Y. "Introductory Training of Academic Reference Librarians: A Survey." *RQ* 26 (Spring 1987), 363–69.

Stanat, Ruth E. "Providing Front Ends for Marketing Executives." *National Online Meeting Proceedings—1988*. Medford, N.J.: Learned Information, 1988.

Stevens, Rolland E. and Walton, Joan M. *Reference Work in the Public Library*. Littleton, Colo.: Libraries Unlimited, 1983.

Stevens, Rolland E. and Smith, Linda C. *Reference Work in the University Library*. Littleton, Colo.: Libraries Unlimited, 1987.

Stewart, Linda and Olsen, Jan. "Compact Disk Databases: Are They Good for Users." *Online* 12 (May 1988), 48–52.

Strozier, Sandra Lynn. "Microsearching Online Catalogs." *Small Computers in Libraries* 7 (September 1987), 40–42.

Tenopir, Carol. "Decision Making by Reference Librarians." *Library Journal* 113 (October 1, 1988), 66–67.

———. "Evaluating Online Systems." *Library Journal* 113 (June 1, 1988), 86–87.

———. "Five Years into the Past . . . Five Years into the Future." *Library Journal* 113 (April 1, 1988), 62–63.

———. "Learning How to Search." *Library Journal* 112 (June 15, 1987), 54–55.

———. "Online Education: Planning for the Future." *Online* 11 (January 1987), 65–66.

———. "Searching by Controlled Vocabulary or Free Text?" *Library Journal* 112 (November 15, 1987), 58–59.

Tschudi, Carol. "The Online Searcher: Education and Training." *Library Hi Tech* (Summer 1983), 85–87.

Vigil, Peter J. *Online Retrieval: Analysis and Strategy.* New York: John Wiley, 1988.

Walker, Geraldine. "The Search Performance of End-Users." *National Online Meeting Proceedings—1988.* Medford, N.J.: Learned Information, 1988.

Watson, Paula D. "Cost to Libraries of the Optical Information Revolution." *Online* 12 (January 1988), 45–50.

Watson, Tom. "A Step Ahead: CD-PAC at the Tacoma Public Library." *Wilson Library Bulletin* 62 (June 1988), 79–81.

White, Marilyn Domas. "Evaluation of the Reference Interview." *RQ* 25 (Fall 1985), 76–84.

White, Herbert S., ed. *Education for Professional Librarians.* White Plains, N.Y.: Knowledge Industry, 1986.

———. "Putting Users to Work." *Library Journal* 113 (March 15, 1988), 40–41.

Wilson, Barbara and Hubbard, Abigail. "Redefining the Role of School Media Specialists . . . Bridging the Gap." *Online* 11 (November 1987), 50–54.

Williams, Martha E. "Highlights of the Online Database Field." *National Online Meeting Proceedings—1988.* Medford, N.J.: Learned Information, 1988.

Wilson, Mark. "How to Set up a Telefascimile Network—The Pennsylvania Libraries' Experience." *Online* 12 (May 1988), 15–25.

Witiak, Joanne. "What is the Role of the Intermediary in End-User Training?" *Online* 12 (September 1988), 50–52.

Yates, Rochelle. *Librarian's Guide to Telephone Reference.* Hamden, Conn.: Library Professional Publications, The Shoe String Press, 1986.

Young, William F. "Methods for Evaluating Reference Desk Performance." *RQ* 25 (Fall 1985), 69–74.

Index

ABI/INFORM, 81; ONDISC, 36
ALANET PLUS, 30
Automated retrieval systems: benefits of, 4–5; and selection guidelines, 22–23
Automated systems and services: selected list of, 26–39

BIBLIO-LINKS, 35
BOOKS IN PRINT, 26, 79
BOOKS IN PRINT PLUS, 25–27, 47, 107
BOOKS OUT OF PRINT PLUS, 27
BRS, 27–28, 58
BRS/AFTER DARK, 25, 27–28, 47, 85
BRS/COLLEAGUE, 28

Case studies, 57–90; and list of sources cited, 90–93
CD-ROM catalogs, 17, 24–25, 74, 79
CD-ROM databases, 22–23
CD-ROM products, 20, 40–41, 47, 50, 62, 67; benefits of, 107; evaluation of, 107–108
Children and youth: motivation of, 20–21; examples of motivation of, 62–63, 67–71, 73–75
CLAIMS/U.S. PATENT ABSTRACTS, 87
College library reference service, 15; examples of, 61–62, 87–88
Community college library reference service, 15; examples of, 59–60
COMPACT DISCLOSURE. *See* DISCLOSURE

COMPREHENSIVE CORE MEDICAL LIBRARY, 58
COMPUSERVE, 30, 61
Computer terminology: glossary of, 42–46

Database systems and services: evaluation of, 106–108
Demonstration disks: use of, 41
DIALOG, 28–29, 57, 63–67, 72–73, 77–81, 84–87; BUSINESS CONNECTION, 28; Classroom Instruction Program, 29; KNOWLEDGE INDEX, 28; MEDICAL CONNECTION, 28; OnDisc, 28
DIALOGLINK, 28
Direct observation. *See* Staff development and training
DISCLOSURE, 29–30, 84; COMPACT, 29
DISCLOSURE/SPECTRUM OWNERSHIP, 84
DISSERTATION ABSTRACTS ONDISC, 37
DOW JONES NEWS/RETRIEVAL, 30

EASYNET, 25, 30–31, 47
Electronic databases: reasons for limiting use of, 2–4
ELECTRONIC ENCYCLOPEDIA, 25, 31; and use as a teaching tool, 67–71
End-user searching: as an option, 53; benefits of, 51, 55–56; quality of, 25, 51, 85–86
End-users: characteristics of, 52–53; education of, 19, 50–56;

End-users (*continued*)
and group/individual instruction for, 55–56; and librarians as consultants for, 55; and library orientation programs for, 54; and trend toward independence of, 50–51
Evaluating reference service. *See* Reference service
Evaluators of reference, 96–97; the staff as, 97–104; end-users as, 104

FACTS ON FILE NEWS DIGEST, 31–32

GEOREF, 63
Glossary. *See* Computer terminology
GRATEFUL MED, 33–34

INFOMASTER, 30
Information specialists, 50; characteristics of ideal, 8–9; and recommended sources for keeping up-to-date, 10–12; and teacher/consultant role of, 53–56
INFOTRAC, 22, 25, 32, 62, 88
In-house files: and use for staff training, 41
Intermediary searching, 50–51, 55; examples of, 62–67, 72–78, 83, 85–86, 88; reasons for reliance on, 25
Interviewing: training staff for, 18–24
IQUEST, 30

LEXIS/NEXIS, 32–33. *See also* NEXIS
LISA, 75–76

MAGAZINE INDEX, 58, 62, 64, 72, 80, 85, 88
MAGAZINE INDEX PLUS, 32
MANAGEMENT CONTENTS, 81
MARC-MATE, 36
Measurement and evaluation of service. *See* Statistical data
MEDLARS, 33–34
MEDLINE, 58, 65, 77, 85–86
MICROCOMPUTER SOFTWARE AND HARDWARE GUIDE, 75

NATIONAL NEWSPAPER INDEX, 62, 64, 72, 80, 85, 88
NEW YORK TIMES ABSTRACTS, 83
NEW YORK TIMES FULL TEXT, 84
NEWSNET, 34
NEWSPAPER ABSTRACTS ONDISC, 37
NEWSEARCH, 62, 64, 80, 88
NEXIS, 57, 83, 90; APOLIT, 59; PAPERS File, 84. *See also* LEXIS/NEXIS
Nonprofessional staff: examples of reference service provided, 61–62, 85, 89; training and evaluation of, 98–100

Older people: reference service to, 21
Online databases: evaluation of, 105–106. *See also* Electronic databases
Online intermediary search service, 17–18; importance of staff development and training in, 25–26; need for, 24–26
Online searching process: outline of, 39–40; and training in, 39–42
ORBIT, 34–35
Orientation and training programs: automated systems and services, 17–18; general, 15–18; and information needed for decisions and referrals, 16–17; and philosophy of service, 15–16; and physical arrangement of the library, 16

PAPERCHASE, 34
Patron online search skills: quality of, 24–26
Peer review, 103. *See also* Evaluators of reference
PERIODICAL ABSTRACTS ONDISC, 37
Personnel needs: and need to examine library responsibility for, 1, 14
PHARMACEUTICAL NEWS INDEX, 85–86
Post-search interview, 23–24. *See also* Interviewing
Print sources: evaluation of, 104–105
PRO-CITE, 35
PRO-SEARCH, 35–36
PSYCINFO, 73, 77
Public library reference service, 15, 20; examples of, 58–60, 63–66, 73–77, 79–83, 87–88, 90

Question negotiation, 20–22

Reference desk activity: examination of, 13–14
Reference interview, 18–24
Reference librarians: types of, 9–10. *See also* Information specialists
Reference service: and children and youth, 20–21, 62–63, 67–71, 73 75; enhanced, 1–6; evaluation of, 94–108; function of, 1–2; and referrals, 16–17, 58–60, 62, 64, 66, 77, 80–81, 84–85, 88–90; and variables that prevent standardization of evaluatory method for, 95–96
Referrals. *See* Reference service
RELIGION INDEX, 72

SCI-MATE, 36; EDITOR, 36; MANAGER, 36
Self-evaluation, 103–104. *See also* Evaluators of reference
Special library reference service, 15–16, 20; and examples of, 65, 71, 73, 77, 80, 86
Staff development and training, 26; direct observation by supervisors, 97–98; and documentation provided, 48–50; and individual and group discussions, 41; and need for, 14–15; and surveys and meetings, 98–100
Statistical data: analysis of, 100–101; importance of, 101–102; and use for evaluating service, 18

TRADE AND INDUSTRY INDEX, 81
TRADEMARKSCAN—FEDERAL and TRADEMARKSCAN—STATE, 66–67
Training programs. *See* Staff development and training; End-users

ULRICH'S PLUS, 27
UMI CD-ROM PRODUCTS, 36–37
University library reference service, 15; and examples of, 84, 88–90

VARIETY'S COMPLETE HOME VIDEO DIRECTORY PLUS, 27
Vendor training and use of videos, 41
VU/TEXT, 37, 82

Williams, Martha, 57
WILSEARCH, 25, 38, 47
WILSONDISC, 38
WILSONLINE, 38

MAR 7 1991